ARNE & CARLOS

Field Guide
to Knitted Birds

OVER 40 HANDMADE PROJECTS TO LIVEN UP YOUR ROOST

Photos: Ragnar Hartvig

TS
TRAFALGAR SQUARE
North Pomfret, Vermont

First published in the United States of
America
in 2017 by
Trafalgar Square Books
North Pomfret, Vermont 05053

Originally published in Norwegian as
Fugler: Fargerike og fantasifulle.

Copyright © 2016 Cappelen Damm AS
English translation © 2017 Trafalgar
Square Books

ISBN: 978-1-64601-071-4

Library of Congress Control Number:
2016963760

Charts: Arne&Carlos
Photography: Ragnar Hartvig
Stylist: Ingrid Skaansar
Book Design: Lise Mosveen
Translator: Carol Huebscher Rhoades

Printed in China

10 9 8 7 6 5 4 3 2 1

CONTENTS

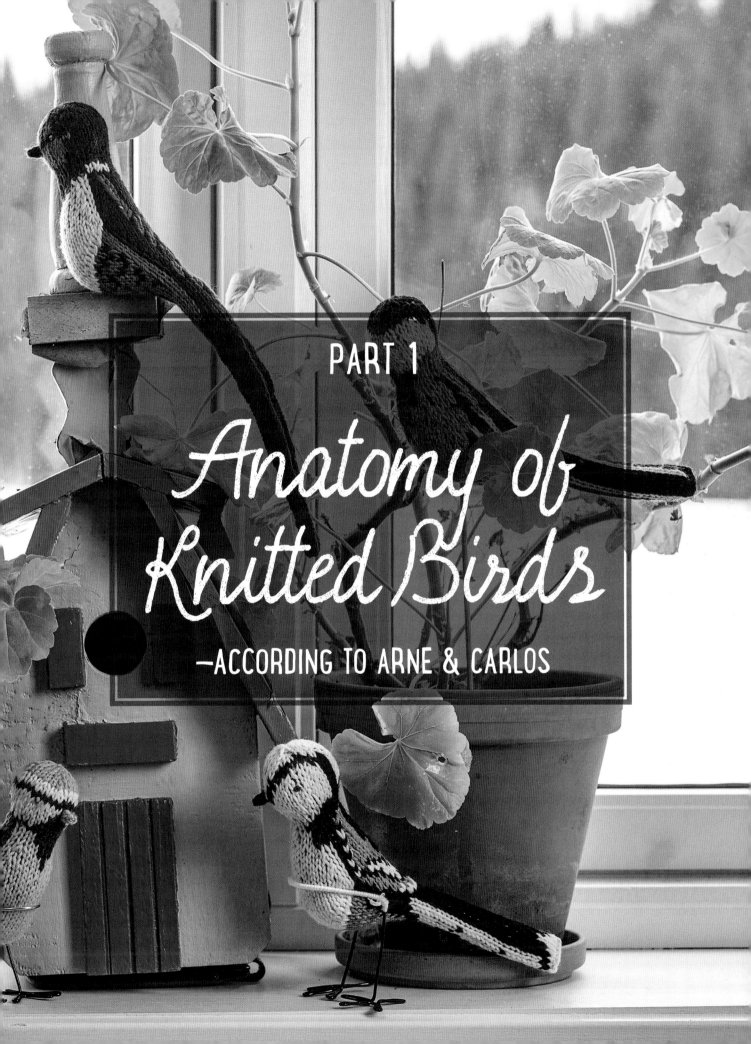

PART 1

Anatomy of Knitted Birds

—ACCORDING TO ARNE & CARLOS

Chapter 1

KNITTING ONE BIRD OR SEVERAL

We both really like birds and do what we can to keep them around. Some of them are here throughout the winter, and are happy to partake of the seeds and bread crumbs that we hang up or set out in bowls and on trays. And when spring comes, we're always happy when we hear our seasonal friends twittering outside our bedroom window for the first time. After the ice and snow melt, we can count on seeing the same pair of red-breasted mergansers that come back year after year to nest in the area around the water near our house. It's always a welcome visit! In the summer, it's showtime when Mom and Dad fly into the birdhouse to feed their young—not to mention the charming spectacle the little ones make when they squeak and peep to make it absolutely clear that they want to have dinner. It's with a certain sadness that we see the migratory birds fly south in the autumn, even if we know they'll faithfully return home in the spring; but we still have our winter bird to keep us company. So we live with birds throughout the year, and they give us much happiness and inspiration.

It hasn't always been that way. In the summer of 2000, when we had just moved into Tonsåsen Station in Etnedal, Valdres, Norway, we found to our great disappointment that we didn't have any birds around the house. When we think back to that time, we realize we shouldn't have been surprised—no one had lived there since 1988, and there was no garden to entice the birds. We did our best to lure the birds back; we built birdhouses and were careful to leave plenty of food in the winter. And, sure enough, they found us eventually!

Our knitted birds started as Christmas decorations. We knitted some to place on a Christmas wreath on the entry door, and then it just developed from there and took over completely! We quickly discovered how much fun it was to knit birds, and we went from knitting single-color birds to some inspired by actual birds. However, we don't rein in our imaginations. We also like to make our own, abstract varieties—we call them designer birds.

So these birds have hats and scarves, traditional motifs, beads, sequins, and even real feathers. The sky's the limit

for what these pretty creations will become—exactly as in nature.

The birds can be used as decorations all year, but many of them have a tendency to roost on the Christmas tree when the time comes. What all the birds have in common is this: they want to give you many hours of happiness. Let loose, try out new color combinations, become inspired, and get going!

Chapter 2

MATERIALS

Getting started is very quick! We're pretty sure most of you already have what you need at home: a little leftover yarn and a set of 5 double-pointed needles. You'll also need a crochet hook the same size as the knitting needles, a little filling to stuff the birds, and, for the eyes, a couple of beads and a needle and thread. That's pretty much it! We specify the needle and hook sizes in each of the patterns.

REGIA DESIGN LINE by ARNE & CARLOS
We have designed 4-ply sock yarn (CYCA #1, 230 yd/210 m / 50 g) from Regia, which has a gauge of 30 stitches and 43 rows in 4 in / 10 cm. It's really fun to use this sock yarn for the birds because they're each so different, and it's always exciting to see the results!

YARN

You can use whatever yarn you like—there isn't a yarn that is right or wrong for these birds. Different types and thick-nesses of yarn can be knitted with different needle sizes to produce different sizes of birds. A display with a collection of several birds in a variety of sizes would be very pretty.

You need about 4 grams of yarn to knit one bird. Since you have to buy a 50-gram ball of each yarn color, we didn't think it was necessary to specify how much yarn you need for each color.

For those of you who want to use the same yarn and colors that we used, we've listed the color numbers in each pattern. If you aren't able to find precisely the same yarn but want to use something similar, visit your local yarn shop. Look for a yarn with the same gauge, quality, and yardage/meterage per 50 grams. The store staff should be able to help you find a good substitute.

We've also collaborated with Schachenmayr to design a self-patterning yarn in 5 different color combinations—also fun to use for the birds. This yarn is part of the Merino Extrafine 120 series.

KNITTING TIPS: If you've never knitted before. we recommend that you begin by knitting single-color birds or using self-patterning yarn. After you've knitted several birds and feel more self-confident, you can try birds worked in two-color stranded knitting. That way, you'll come to understand the patterns better and can focus more on the chart and less on the text.

COTTON YARN

The birds can also be knitted with 100% cotton yarn if you prefer. We knitted a few birds in Catania from Schachenmayr. Catania has one of the largest color selections we've seen and the colors are so beautiful and so varied! A 50-gram ball has about 137 yards / 125 meters and knits to a gauge of 26 stitches and 36 rows in 4 in / 10 cm.

What about some exciting yarn for birds for the Christmas tree? Knit them in all possible color combinations and then decorate them with sequins and glittery yarn. We used Anchor Metallic Embroidery thread to embroider the bird at the far left. You'll find the patterns for the Titmouse on page 75, the Blue Tit on page 77, and the Wagtail on page 83.

With Anchor's enormous color selection, the color combinations are endless. Only your imagination sets the limits on what your birds can look like.

EMBROIDERY YARN

The birds of paradise are a little smaller than the birds knitted with Merino or sock yarn. These were inspired by hummingbirds and we gave up trying to find as fine a yarn as we wanted. For that reason, we chose to knit them with Anchor Mouliné 6-ply embroidery thread (100% cotton). We used needles U.S. size 000 / 1.5 mm for this yarn and the birds have a gauge of 30 stitches and 40 rounds in 4 in / 10 cm. DMC offers the same colors and you can find a conversion chart on the internet.

BEADS, SEQUINS, AND FEATHERS

Hobby shops usually have a good selection of beads, sequins, and crystals that you can decorate the birds with. Only your imagination will limit how spectacular the birds of paradise can be once you start embellishing! If you don't want to sit and slowly sew on beads or sequins, you can, instead, use strings of sequins which are quicker. However, we must say, we think the results are amazing when you sew the sequins on one by one so they are tightly spaced and overlap each other, making a pretty, feather-like effect.

We have also chosen to use beads for the eyes on all the birds. Choose a color that contrasts well so the eyes will be very visible. 8/0 glass seed beads are a good option.

You can also find pretty feathers at hobby shops and can use them to make wings and tails for the birds.

FILLING

We've used various materials for filling the birds, such as acrylic pillow stuffing but we most like Rauma's carded wool or Hillesvåg's 100% carded wool. Calculate on about ¾ oz / 20 g per bird.

TIP: If you have some wool yarn leftovers or yarn tails from all your knitting and crochet projects, you can card them and use the little batts for filling—this works just well as carded wool and you'll save a little money.

MATERIALS FOR THE GLASSES AND STANDS

The glasses frames are formed with fine steel wire (the type used for floral decorations) and then the desired color of yarn is wrapped around the frames. We used Biltema super glue for metal. The claws are shaped with galvanized steel wire and dipped in Bengalack (a universal varnish for metal, wood, and hard plastic). You can also sew old Christmas light holders or small clothes pins to the birds. To hold the birds in flower pots and with floral decorations, a grill skewer or a fine florist's skewer will work well.

A LITTLE ABOUT GAUGE FOR THE BIRDS

Gauge is even more important than yarn choice for the birds. That's because you have to stuff the birds and the gauge cannot be so loose that the filling shows through. We recommend that you go down a needle size if you knit loosely. In our instructions, we adjusted the recommended gauge for the yarns we used. You can go to the yarn store and easily find substitutes for these yarn qualities if you want. However, it is important to emphasize that the recommended yarn gauge isn't the gauge as for our birds. We went down in needle size and knitted much more tightly so that the filling won't show through. It's always a good idea to knit a little gauge swatch first, to make sure of your own gauge. Our birds, no matter what yarn, have a gauge of about 30 stitches and 40 rounds in 4 in / 10 cm. You can find more information about gauge in the Basic Pattern in Chapter 3.

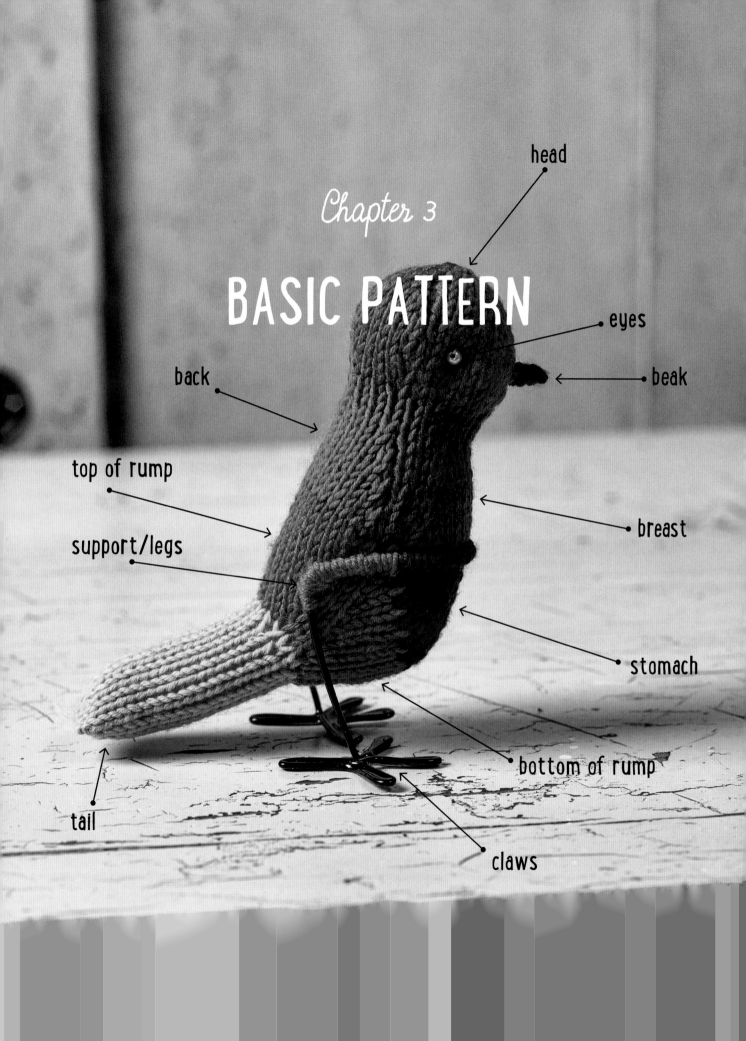

Chapter 3

BASIC PATTERN

head

eyes

beak

back

top of rump

support/legs

breast

stomach

bottom of rump

tail

claws

HOW TO KNIT FROM THE CHARTS WITHOUT READING THE PATTERN TEXT EACH TIME

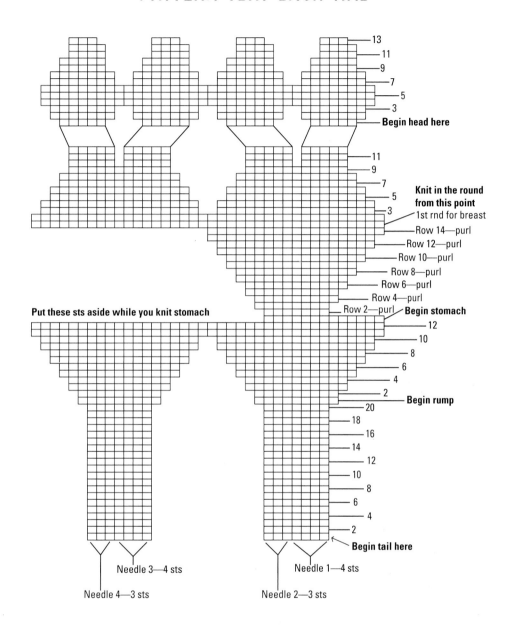

Begin head here

13
11
9
7
5
3

11
9
7
5
3

Knit in the round from this point

1st rnd for breast

Row 14—purl
Row 12—purl
Row 10—purl
Row 8—purl
Row 6—purl
Row 4—purl
Row 2—purl

Begin stomach

12
10
8
6
4
2

Begin rump

Put these sts aside while you knit stomach

20
18
16
14
12
10
8
6
4
2

Begin tail here

Needle 3—4 sts
Needle 4—3 sts
Needle 1—4 sts
Needle 2—3 sts

ABBREVIATIONS

BO   bind off (= British cast off)
ch   chain
cm   centimeter(s)
CO   cast on
dc   double crochet (= British treble crochet)
dpn   double-pointed needles
in   inch(es)
inc   increase
k   knit
k2tog   knit 2 stitches together

M1   make one: lift strand between 2 stitches and knit into back loop
m   meter(s)
mm   millimeter(s)
ndl(s) needle(s)
p   purl
RLI   right lifted increase: knit into right side of st below first stitch on needle
rem   remain(s)(ing)
rep   repeat
rnd(s) round(s)

RS   right side
sc   single crochet (= British double crochet)
sl   slip
st(s)   stitch(es)
WS   wrong side
yd   yard(s)
yo   yarnover

INCREASING: You can increase with M1 between stitches, k1f&b (knit into front and then back of same stitch), or with RLI.

21

BASIC PATTERN

Needles: U.S. size 0-2.5 / 2-3 mm, set of 5 dpn

TAIL:

CO *14 sts and divide over 4 dpn: 4 + 3 + 4 + 3 sts.* Knit 20 rnds.

NOTE: Make sure the floats on the WS don't pull in when knitting birds with a pattern on the tail. As you knit, periodically use your index finger to stretch out the "tube" for the tail. Also make sure the stitches lie smoothly next to each other. If you pull too tightly when knitting the pattern, the contrast color stitches can become quite small or disappear altogether between the main color stitches. After completing the tail, insert a pen or pencil into the tail and use it to smooth the stitches out.

RUMP:

Shape the rump by increasing at the sides. Work stitches within parentheses 2 times per round.
Rnd 1: (K1, inc 1, k5, inc 1, k1) around.
Rnd 2: K18.
Rnd 3: (K1, inc 1, k7, inc 1, k1) around.
Rnd 4: K22.
Rnd 5: (K1, inc 1, k9, inc 1, k1) around.
Rnd 6: K26.
Rnd 7: (K1, inc 1, k11, inc 1, k1) around.
Rnd 8: K30.
Rnd 9: (K1, inc 1, k13, inc 1, k1) around.
Rnd 10: K34.
Rnd 11: (K1, inc 1, k15, inc 1, k1) around.
Rnd 12: K38.

STOMACH:

Work back and forth in short rows, with knit over knit and purl over purl as stitches face you.
Always slip the first stitch purlwise with yarn in back on RS and yarn in front on WS.
Row 1: K13; turn.
Row 2: Sl 1, p6; turn.
Row 3: Sl 1, k7; turn.
Row 4: Sl 1, p8; turn.
Row 5: Sl 1, k9; turn.
Row 6: Sl 1, p10; turn.
Row 7: Sl 1, k11; turn.
Row 8: Sl 1, p12; turn.
Row 9: Sl 1, k13; turn.
Row 10: Sl 1, p14; turn.
Row 11: Sl 1, k15; turn.
Row 12: Sl 1, p16; turn.
Row 13: Sl 1, k17; turn.
Row 14: Sl 1, p18; turn.
Now return to knitting in the round.

BREAST:

The breast is shaped by decreasing at the sides. Work stitches within parentheses 2 times per round.
Rnd 1: Sl 1, k37.
Rnd 2: K38.
Rnd 3: (K1, k2tog, k13, k2tog, k1) around.
Rnd 4: K34.
Rnd 5: (K1, k2tog, k11, k2tog, k1) around.
Rnd 6: K30.
Rnd 7: (K1, k2tog, k9, k2tog, k1) around.
Rnd 8: K26.
Rnd 9: (K1, k2tog, k7, k2tog, k1) around = 22 sts rem.
Rnd 10: (K4, k2tog, k5) around.
Rnd 11: K20.
Rnd 12: K20.

HEAD:

Repeat stitches within parentheses 4 times around.
Rnd 1: K20.
Rnd 2: (K1, inc 1, k3, inc 1, k1) around.
Rnd 3: K28.
Rnd 4: (K1, inc 1, k5, inc 1, k1) around.
Rnd 5: K36.
Rnd 6: K36.
Rnd 7: (K1, k2tog, k3, k2tog, k1) around.
Rnd 8: K28.
Rnd 9: (K1, k2tog, k1, k2tog, k1) around.
Rnd 10: K20.
Rnd 11: (K1, k2tog, k2) around.
Rnd 12: K16.
Rnd 13: (K1, k2tog, k1) around.

Cut yarn and draw end through remaining 12 sts.
Sew the tail together flat at the cast-on row, making sure the top and bottom sides lie correctly.
Fill with wool or pillow stuffing. You can also use the yarn ends from the birds or other projects, card them, and then use the "batting" as filling for the knitted birds.
Tighten the yarn holding final stitches of the head.
Weave in any ends to inside of bird.
Crochet the beak (see details on pages 26-27).
Now you can decorate the bird with duplicate stitching if necessary.

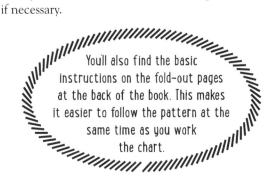

You'll also find the basic instructions on the fold-out pages at the back of the book. This makes it easier to follow the pattern at the same time as you work the chart.

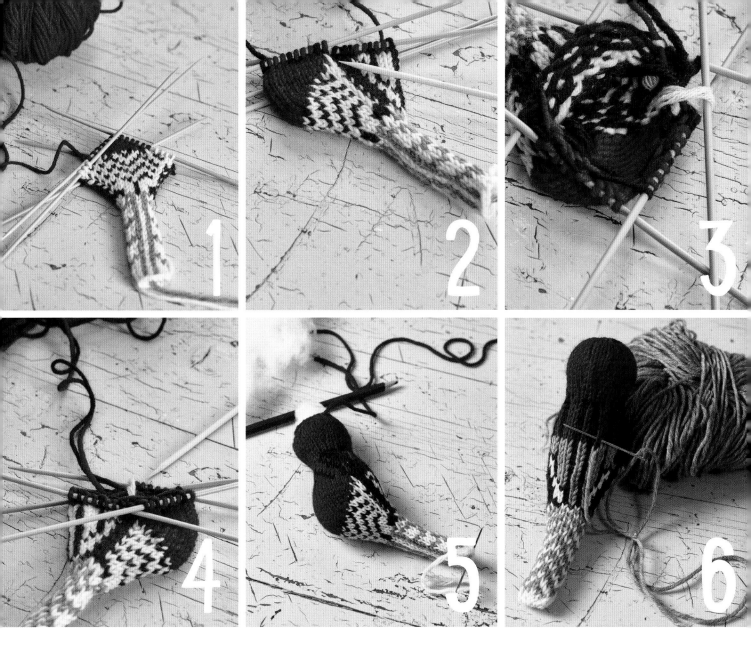

1   After the tail has been completely knitted, insert a pencil into the tail and press it around to smooth out the stitches. The stomach is worked back and forth with knit and purl short rows, as for the heel turn on a sock.

2   Check to make sure the stitches on the stomach are not too loose. The stitches from turning and working back on knit and purl rows can sometimes be a little loose.

3   We tighten up any loose stitches and then cut any long strands so we can then knot them together, or for any very long strands, we let them hang until we can pick them up onto the needle on the next round to knit together with a stitch.

4   When there are some long strands after we've tightened the knitting, we knit them together with a stitch. We always start the round by knitting the long strand together with the first stitch. If you lift the strand onto the needle and knit it together with the last stitch on the round, it will be visible on the right side.

5   Fill the bird with wool or pillow stuffing. You can also use yarn tails from the birds or other projects, card the yarn, and then use the batting as filling for the knitted birds.

6   Now you can decorate the bird with duplicate stitch if necessary.

DUPLICATE STITCH

1 You can embroider with duplicate stitch over already-knit stitches to add new colors. Use a tapestry needle with a blunt tip and bring the yarn through at the base of the stitch you will embroider over. Sew under the two legs of the stitch above the one you are covering.

2 Insert the needle down at the same place where you brought it through at the beginning—that is, at the base of the stitch you are covering. *At the same time,* bring the needle out again at the base of the next stitch to be covered.

3 Bring the yarn through, making sure it doesn't pull in too much.

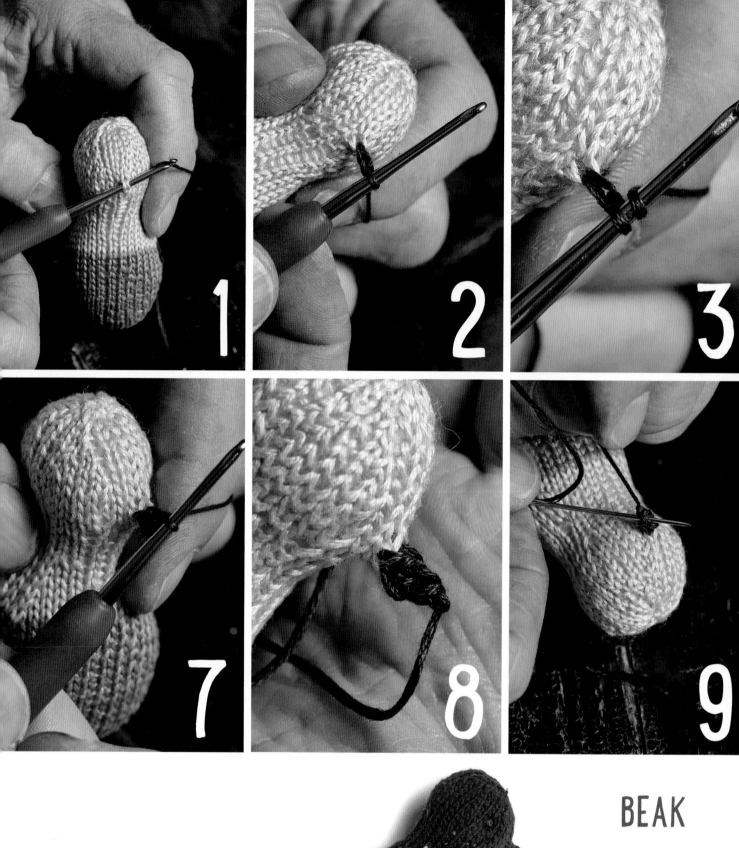

BEAK

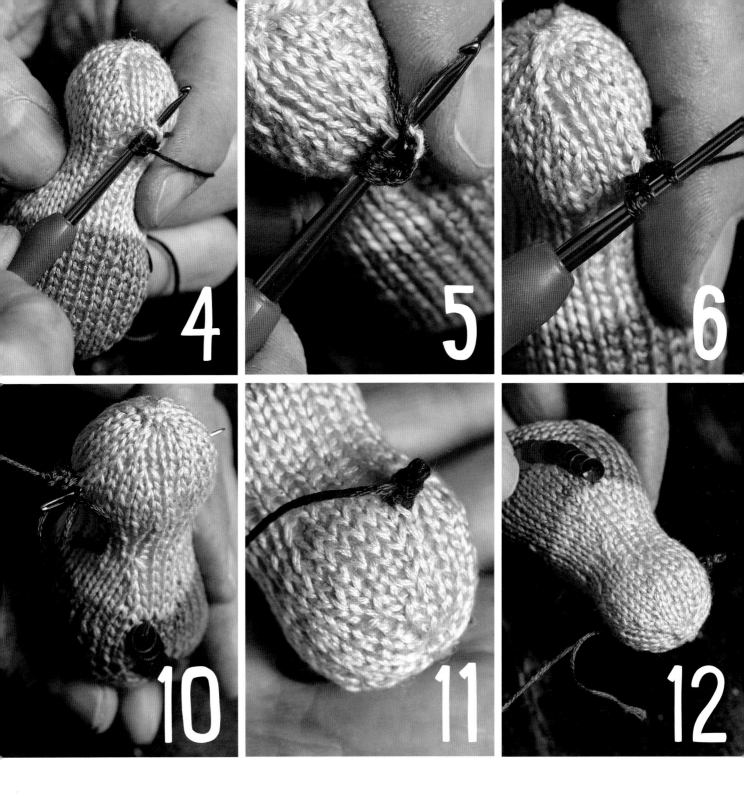

Crochet 3 dc together (3-dc cluster) / British 3 tr together (3-tr cluster) as follows:

Begin with ch 2 around a stitch at the center of the face.

For the first dc / tr: Yarn around hook, insert hook into the 1st st up from one side of the first ch and through the nearest strand of the st above. Yarn around hook and through 2 loops.

Second dc / tr: Yarn around hook, insert hook into st above ch, yarn around hook and through first 2 loops on hook.

Third dc / tr: Yarn around hook, insert hook into st on opposite side of ch, yarn around hook and through first 2 loops on hook.

Yarn around hook and bring through remaining loops on hook all at once.

End the beak by cutting yarn and drawing the end through the last st of the 3-dc / 3-tr cluster.

Use the two yarn ends to sew back and forth through the beak to make it stronger. Thread the ends through the head and fasten off.

1

EYES

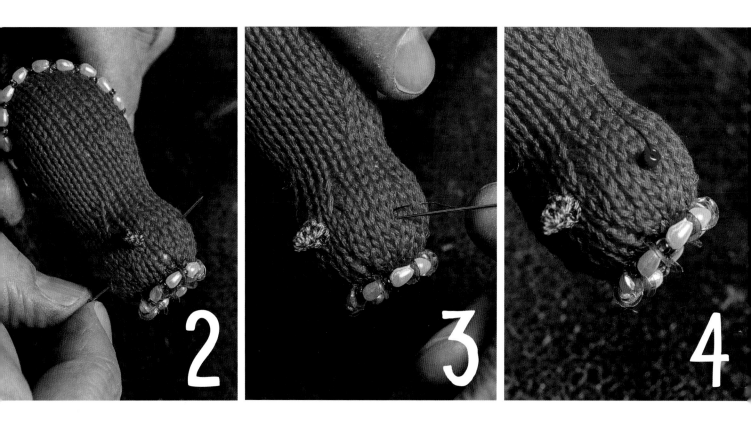

Sew on two beads, one on each side of the head. You will need a size 9 or 10 beading needle, rather than a regular sewing needle, to fit through most small beads. First attach one bead with a stitch and then bring the needle through the head over to the opposite side where you will place the second eye. Sew back and forth through the beads and then down on the outside of each bead until they sit smoothly on the head.

GLASSES

You'll need steel wire, super glue and yarn in the same color as the frame.

Shape the frames with fine steel wire (the type used for floral decorations). Begin with the first arm of the glasses, bend the wire toward the lenses and form them into the shape you want. At the end piece (at the bend between the arm and the top bar), bend the wire down to and across the bottom of the lens, up to the nose and back to the top bar. Wrap the wire for the top bar above the lens and then over to the second lens. Start with the top bar, shaping the top, side, and then the bottom of the lens, and then up to the nose before you twist the wire for the top bar of the lens. End with the second arm. Smooth out the glasses one last time. Reinforce with super glue on the end piece of the first arm, and then at all the places where the frame made a turn. With the color you want, wrap wool yarn around the frame. You need glue that can be used on metal—protect your fingers because this glue is strong.

SUPPORTS FOR THE BIRDS

Galvanized steel wire, 1.5 mm

Universal varnish

Pliers

Dowel

Super glue for metal

Each leg has four claws

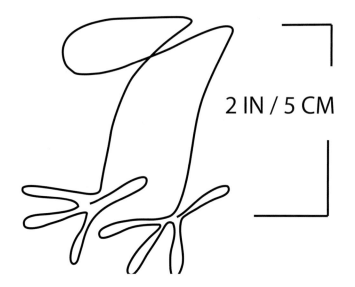

2 IN / 5 CM

Mass production of bird legs

HERE'S HOW TO MAKE THE SUPPORTS

   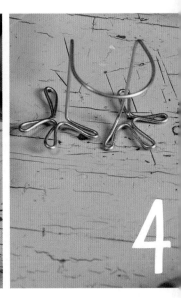

1 Begin at the end of the steel wire with the left foot. Place the pliers ⅝ in / 1.5 cm up from the bottom of the steel wire, bend the wire, and clamp the piece together carefully. You've made the back claw. Make the three front claws by bending and clamping the wire. Shape the claws so they all smoothly point in the correct direction, one at the back and three front claws fanning out on the other side.

2 Bend the steel wire so it is perpendicular to the front claws and is centered behind the three claws that point forward. To form the bowed brace for the stomach, we used a broom handle, marking a point on the shaft that fits the stomachs of our birds. Place the steel wire on the point you have marked, about 1¼ in / 3 cm from the bend over the leg, and shape the wire around the broom shaft or a round dowel. If you've used a round dowel, you don't need to mark it.

3 Eyeball the measurement and bend the steel wire down again so the bow shape you made around the dowel looks even on both sides of the legs. Check to make sure the legs are the same length. Ours are about 2 in / 5 cm long.

4 Bend the wire into the four claws for the right foot, as you did for the left foot. When you've formed the fourth claw (the one that points backwards, this time), cut off any excess wire and clamp it. Shape the four claws so they lie flat, three pointing forwards and one backwards, and so the legs will stand level on a tabletop.

PAINTING THE SUPPORT

If you want to paint the support, it's best if you just dip the legs individually into a can of varnish. Let the varnish drip off and turn the support so the varnish doesn't clump up. Have some paper at the ready in case you need to remove a few drops. Leave the support upside down to dry.

When the support has dried, you can work single crochet / British double crochet starting with about ⅜ in / 1 cm on top of the left leg, across the bowed stomach brace, and then down about ⅜ / 1 cm on the right leg. Use one or two of the colors in the bird where the bow comes over the rump and stomach. Or you can attach thread with super glue around the steel wire from the top of one leg, across the bow, to the top of the other leg. You can also attach the support to the bird with the same yarn colors the steel wire lies over, or just leave the metal plain.

With a tree branch and a lot of birds, you can bring spring into the cottage and create a lovely atmosphere in your home.

PART 2

The Birds

Chapter 4

WINTER BIRDS

These are easy birds to knit. You can adjust the hat sizes by knitting with various needle sizes. Crochet the beak and sew on the hat before you add the eyes. Characteristics: Single-color birds with a hat and scarf or a hat with a pompom. These birds flock to the Christmas tree on the night before Christmas eve. The colorful accessories set winter birds apart from other birds!

CHARACTERISTICS: In folk traditions these are referred to as "those who can't keep warm," because they are the world's only birds with both scarves and hats. Nevertheless, they can be found even in the polar region.

OLA and KARI

MATERIALS

Yarn: CYCA #3 (DK weight) Schachenmayr Merino Extrafine 120 DK, 100% wool (131 yd/120 m / 50 g)
Color: White 00101 and small amount of Dark Blue (from scarf) for the beak
Needles: U.S. size 0-2.5 / 2-3 mm, set of 5 dpn
Gauge: 30 sts and 40 rnds in 4 x 4 in / 10 x 10 cm.
Adjust needle size to obtain correct gauge if necessary.

BIRD

CO 14 sts and divide onto 4 dpn: 4 + 3 + 4 + 3. Join to work in the round. Work following the Basic Pattern on page 22.

After completing head, cut yarn and draw end through rem 12 sts. Flatten the tail and sew the end at the cast-on row, making sure that the top and bottom sides are correctly oriented. Stretch the body well and tighten any stitches that are too loose.
Block by gently steam pressing under a damp pressing cloth. Fill the bird and sew the hole at top of head to close.
Crochet the beak: Work a 3-dc cluster (see page 27). Use one of the hat colors for the beak.

Single-color birds are more flexible than birds with color patterns, so you can shape them to your liking as you fill them.
Make the hats for the birds.

HAT WITH POMPOM

MATERIALS

Yarn: CYCA #3 (DK weight) Schachenmayr Merino Extrafine 120 DK, 100% wool (131 yd/120 m / 50 g)

Colors:
Version 1: Light Gray 00190 (Color 1), Red 00131 (Color 2)
Version 2: Light Blue 00152 (Color 1), Dark Blue 00153 (Color 2)
Needles: U.S. sizes 1.5 and 2.5 / 2.5 and 3 mm, set of 5 dpn

With smaller needles and Color 1, CO 24 sts. Divide evenly onto 4 dpn = 6 sts per needle; join to knit in the round.
Work 5 rnds k2, p2 ribbing.
Change to larger needles and work following the chart.
Rnds 1-4: K24.
Rnd 5: Work (k2tog, k2) around.
Rnd 6: K18.
Rnd 7: Work (k2tog, k1) around.
Rnd 8: K12.
Cut yarn and draw end through rem 12 sts. Weave in ends neatly on WS.

Make a small pompom with the contrast color, about ⅝ in / 16 mm diameter. Sew the pompom to the top of the hat and then sew hat to bird's head. A single-color bird can see in all directions, so place the hat sitting correctly in relation to the direction you want the bird to look. Sew on the eyes.

color version 1

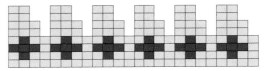

color version 2

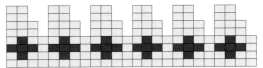

SCARF

MATERIALS

Yarn: CYCA #3 (DK weight) Schachenmayr Merino Extrafine 120 DK, 100% wool (131 yd/120 m / 50 g)
Colors:
Version 1: Light Gray 00190
Version 2: Light Blue 00152
Needles: U.S. size 2.5 / 3 mm, 2 dpn or straights

CO 7 sts and work back and forth in garter st. We made our scarves 8 in / 20 cm long. The bird with the gray and red hat has a Light Gray scarf. The bird with the blue hat has a matching Light Blue 00152 scarf.

Because winter birds are only one color, you can make the beak point in whichever direction you like. Sew the hat on so it faces the same direction as the head.

CHARACTERISTICS: Because the Peruvian hat fits the face closely, Juanita's eyes are closer together than the eyes on other birds.

CHARACTERISTICS: Large hats with colorful pompoms on the tops and hanging at the breast from the earflap cords. They nest in dense spruce forests in eastern Norway, and their easily recognizable song can be confused with Abba's Chiquitita on the pan flute. Winter birds can be found both north and south of the equator. These are dressed in Peruvian-style accessories. You'll find the pattern for the birds on page 41.

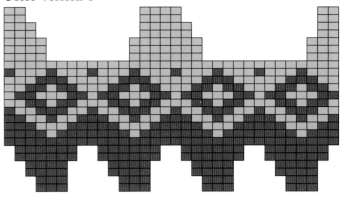

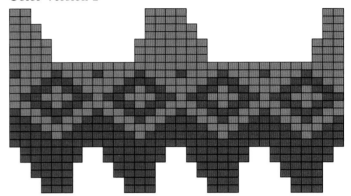

PEDRO and JUANITA

PERUVIAN HAT

MATERIALS

Yarn: CYCA #3 (DK weight) Schachenmayr Merino Extrafine 120 DK, 100% wool (131 yd/120 m / 50 g)
Colors:
Version 1: Green 00170, Red 00131, Yellow 00121, Pink 00137
Version 2: Red 00131, Purple 00146, Blue 00165, Yellow 00121
Needles: U.S. size 2.5 / 3 mm, set of 5 dpn
Crochet Hook: U.S. size D-3 / 3 mm

CO 12 sts and divide evenly onto 4 dpn = 3 sts per needle.
Rnd 1: K12.
Rnd 2: (K1, inc 1, k2) around.
Rnd 3: K16.
Rnd 4: (K1, inc 1, k2, inc 1, k1) around.
Rnd 5: K24.
Rnd 6: (K1, inc 1, k4, inc 1, k1) around.
Rnds 7-16: K32 following the chart.
Rnd 17: K3, BO 10 sts, k7, including last st after bind-off, BO 8, k4, including last st after bind-off. On next rnd, k3; turn and work first earflap over 7 sts and put rem 7 sts on holder for second earflap.
Row 1: Sl 1, p6.
Row 2: Sl 1, k6.
Row 3: Sl 1, p6.
Row 4: Sl 1, k2tog, k1, k2tog, k1.
Row 5: Sl 1, p4.

Row 6: Sl 1, k2tog, k2.
Row 7: Sl 1, p3.
BO rem sts and cut yarn.

Slip the 7 held sts to needle and then make the other earflap the same way.
Weave in all ends neatly on WS. Sew hole at top of hat and then, with yellow or blue, work single crochet / British double crochet all around the edge, including earflaps. For each earflap, ch 7 with same color as sc / dc edging. Make 3 small pompoms and sew one to the top of the hat and one onto end of each cord. The pompoms shown here are pink and yellow, ⅝ in / 16 mm and ½ in / 12 mm in diameter.

Chapter 5

EMBROIDERED BIRDS

We found some old Mexican women's magazines at an antique market in Mexico City. The magazines had pretty colorful pages with pattern charts for embroidery and we couldn't resist them. They came home with us to Valdres. We took the inspiration for the embroidery on these birds from the old pattern pages. None of our embroidery matches the originals exactly. Since the tail doesn't have more than 7 x 2 stitches, there is very little space for decorating. The birds were knitted in one color following the Basic Pattern, blocked, and stuffed with filling before we embroidered the various motifs.

CHARACTERISTICS: The yellow bird is knitted following the Basic Pattern on page 22. It is embroidered with duplicate stitch with dark pink, light pink, and purple yarn.

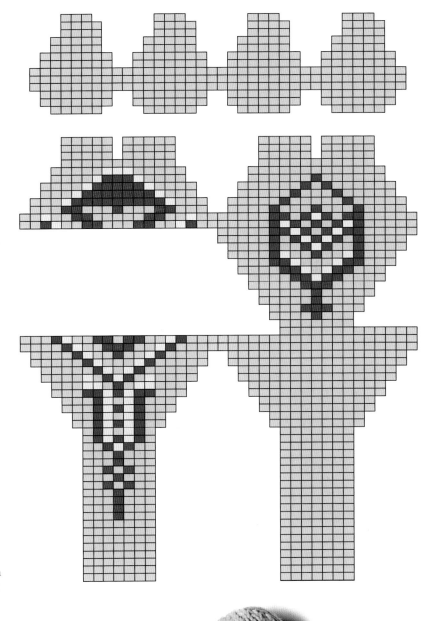

PANCHO

MATERIALS

Yarn: CYCA #3 (DK weight) Schachenmayr
Merino Extrafine 120 DK, 100% wool (131
yd/120 m / 50 g)
Colors: Yellow 00121, Dark Pink 00138,
Light Pink 00135, Purple 00147
Needles: U.S. size 0-2.5 / 2-3 mm, set of 5 dpn
Gauge: 30 sts and 40 rnds in 4 x 4 in / 10 x 10
cm. Adjust needle size to obtain correct gauge
if necessary.

*With Yellow, CO 14 sts and divide onto 4 dpn: 4 + 3 + 4 +
3. Join to work in the round. Work following the Basic
Pattern on page 22 and the chart on this page.*

Place markers on the center stitch on the back and center
stitch of the breast to make it easier to begin the embroidery motifs after the bird has been knitted and filled.

Flatten the tail and sew the end at the cast-on row,
making sure that the top and bottom sides are correctly
oriented. Stretch the body well and tighten any stitches
that are too loose.
Block by gently steam pressing under a damp pressing
cloth. Fill the bird and sew the hole at top of head to
close.

Single-color birds are more flexible
than birds with color patterns, so you
can shape them to your liking as you fill them.
Embroider the motifs with duplicate stitch.
Crochet the beak and sew on the eyes. Our bird has a
purple beak and dark blue eyes.

KNITTING TIP: Bring an old bird cage back to life with knitted birds: easy pets that only need a little care.

KNITTING TIP: Knit a pin cushion and decorate it with a bird. Our cushion is made of four strips knitted back and forth in garter stitch.

PIN CUSHION

MATERIALS

Yarn: CYCA #3 (DK weight) Schachenmayr Merino Extrafine 120 DK, 100% wool (131 yd/120 m / 50 g)
Color: Dark Pink 00138, 50 g
Needles: U.S. size 2.5 / 3 mm, 2 dpn

CO 24 sts and knit 28 ridges (2 rows = 1 ridge). BO.
CO 20 sts and knit 38 ridges. BO.
CO 16 sts and knit 48 ridges. BO.
CO 12 sts and knit 58 ridges. BO.

When you count the ridges, check to be sure that the cast-on tail is at the right side (with RS facing). When you've knitted all the ridges, the bind-off tail will be at the left side. Hold piece with RS facing you. With RS facing RS, seam the cast-on and bind-off edges into a circle. Working on a flat surface, fold the strips lengthwise with the side stitches down on the table. Arrange the strips like a stacked puzzle with the 28-ridge strip at the inside and the 58-ridge strip on the outside.

CHARACTERISTICS: The orange bird is knitted following the Basic Pattern on page 22 and then embroidered with dark green and white.

FRIDA

MATERIALS

Yarn: CYCA #3 (DK weight) Schachenmayr Merino Extrafine 120 DK, 100% wool (131 yd/120 m / 50 g)
Colors: Orange 00125, Dark Green 00172, White 00101
Needles: U.S. size 0-2.5 / 2-3 mm, set of 5 dpn
Gauge: 30 sts and 40 rnds in 4 x 4 in / 10 x 10 cm.
Adjust needle size to obtain correct gauge if necessary.

With Orange, CO 14 sts and divide onto 4 dpn: 4 + 3 + 4 + 3. Join to work in the round. Work following the Basic Pattern on page 22 and the chart on this page.

Place markers on the first stitch of the tail and first stitch of the breast to make it easier to begin the embroidery motifs after the bird has been knitted and filled.

Stretch the body well and tighten any stitches that are too loose.
Flatten the tail and sew the end at the cast-on row, making sure that the top and bottom sides are correctly oriented.
Single-color birds are more flexible than birds with color patterns, so you can shape them to your liking as you fill them.
Block by gently steam pressing under a damp pressing cloth. Fill the bird and sew the hole at top of head to close.
Embroider the motifs with duplicate stitch.
Crochet the beak and sew on the eyes. Our bird has a green beak and light green eyes.

53

CHARACTERISTICS: The blue bird is knitted following the Basic Pattern on page 22 and then embroidered with pink and dark pink.

DIEGO

MATERIALS

Yarn: CYCA #3 (DK weight) Schachenmayr Merino Extrafine 120 DK, 100% wool (131 yd/120 m / 50 g)
Colors: Royal Blue 00151, Dark Pink 00138, Light Pink 00135 + small amount of Red for beak
Needles: U.S. size 0-2.5 / 2-3 mm, set of 5 dpn
Gauge: 30 sts and 40 rnds in 4 x 4 in / 10 x 10 cm.
Adjust needle size to obtain correct gauge if necessary.

With Blue, CO 14 sts and divide onto 4 dpn: 4 + 3 + 4 + 3. Join to work in the round. Work following the Basic Pattern on page 22 and the chart on this page.

Place markers on the first stitch of the tail and first stitch of the breast to make it easier to begin the embroidery motifs after the bird has been knitted and filled.

Flatten the tail and sew the end at the cast-on row, making sure that the top and bottom sides are correctly oriented. Stretch the body well and tighten any stitches that are too loose.
Single-color birds are more flexible than birds with color patterns, so you can shape them to your liking as you fill them.
Block by gently steam pressing under a damp pressing cloth. Fill the bird and sew the hole at top of head to close.
Embroider the motifs with duplicate stitch.
Crochet the beak and sew on the eyes. Our bird has a red beak and red eyes.

A bird in the hand. The old saint has been brightened up with a blue bird.

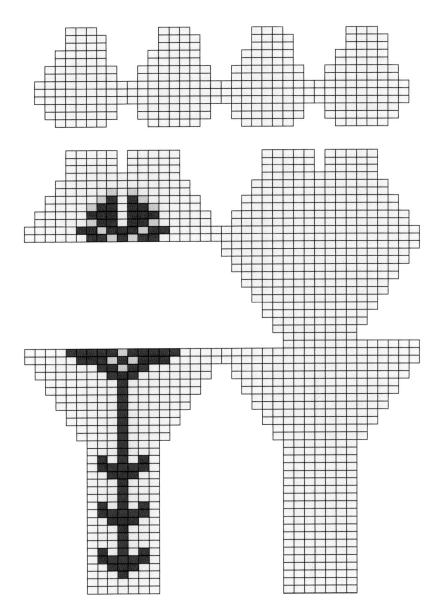

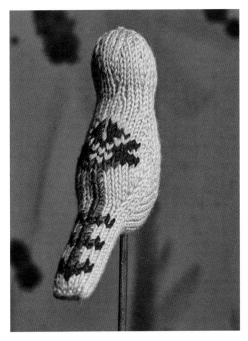

CHARACTERISTICS: *This light blue bird has been knitted following the Basic Pattern on page 22 and then embroidered with green, red, and yellow on its back, rump, and tail.*

SANTOS

MATERIALS

Yarn: CYCA #3 (DK weight) Schachenmayr Merino Extrafine 120 DK, 100% wool (131 yd/120 m / 50 g)
Colors: Light Blue 00165, Green 00172, Red 00131, Yellow 00121
Needles: U.S. size 0-2.5 / 2-3 mm, set of 5 dpn
Gauge: 30 sts and 40 rnds in 4 x 4 in / 10 x 10 cm. Adjust needle size to obtain correct gauge if necessary.

With Light Blue, CO 14 sts and divide onto 4 dpn: 4 + 3 + 4 + 3. Join to work in the round. Work following the Basic Pattern on page 22 and the chart on this page.

Place a marker on the first stitch of the tail to make it easier to begin the embroidery motifs after the bird has been knitted and filled.

Flatten the tail and sew the end at the cast-on row, making sure that the top and bottom sides are correctly oriented. Stretch the body well and tighten any stitches that are too loose.

Single-color birds are more flexible than birds with color patterns, so you can shape them to your liking as you fill them.

Block by gently steam pressing under a damp pressing cloth. Fill the bird and sew the hole at top of head to close.

Embroider the motifs with duplicate stitch.

Crochet the beak and sew on the eyes. Our bird has a red beak and red eyes.

CHARACTERISTICS: A mint-green bird knitted following the Basic Pattern on page 22 and embroidered in green, blue, and red.

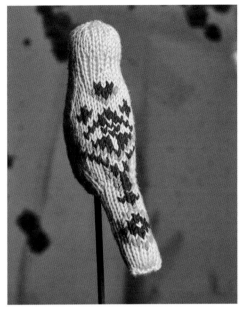

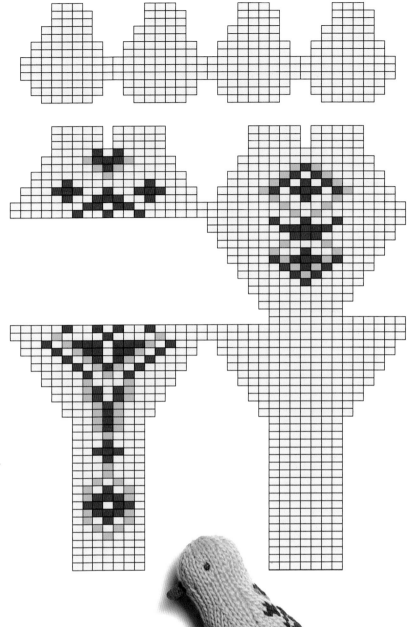

KNITTING TIP: Make three pompoms with the same colors as for the embroidered motifs on the bird. Twist three cords and knot them at the ends. Sew the cords with their pompoms to the bird's stomach and then twist a cord to sew to the back of the bird.

DOLORES

MATERIALS

Yarn: CYCA #3 (DK weight) Schachenmayr Merino Extrafine 120 DK, 100% wool (131 yd/120 m / 50 g)
Colors: Mint Green 00167, Green 00174, Red 00131, Blue 00153
Needles: U.S. size 0-2.5 / 2-3 mm, set of 5 dpn
Gauge: 30 sts and 40 rnds in 4 x 4 in / 10 x 10 cm. Adjust needle size to obtain correct gauge if necessary.

With Mint Green, CO 14 sts and divide onto 4 dpn: 4 + 3 + 4 + 3. Join to work in the round. Work following the Basic Pattern on page 22 and the chart on this page.

Places markers on the first stitch of the tail and first stitch of the breast to make it easier to begin the embroidery motifs after the bird has been knitted and filled.

Flatten the tail and sew the end at the cast-on row, making sure that the top and bottom sides are correctly oriented. Stretch the body well and tighten any stitches that are too loose. Single-color birds are more flexible than birds with color patterns, so you can shape them to your liking as you fill them.
Block by gently steam pressing under a damp pressing cloth. Fill the bird and sew the hole at top of head to close.
Embroider the motifs with duplicate stitch.
Crochet the beak and sew on the eyes. Our bird has a red beak and red eyes.

CHARACTERISTICS: This light blue bird is knitted following the Basic Pattern on page 22 and embroidered in purple, pink, and red.

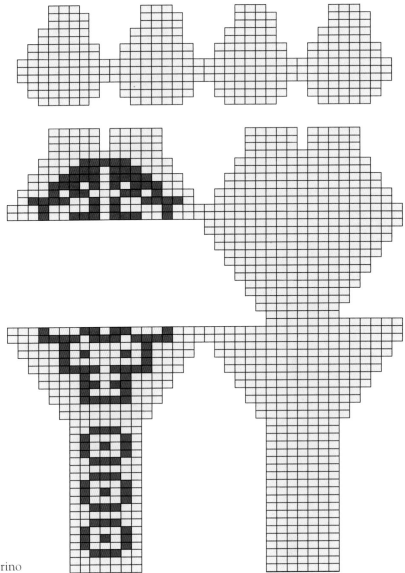

MANUEL

MATERIALS

Yarn: CYCA #3 (DK weight) Schachenmayr Merino
Extrafine 120 DK, 100% wool (131 yd/120 m / 50 g)
Colors: Light Blue 00152, Purple 00147, Pink 00135,
Red 00131
Needles: U.S. size 0-2.5 / 2-3 mm, set of 5 dpn
Gauge: 30 sts and 40 rnds in 4 x 4 in / 10 x 10 cm.
Adjust needle size to obtain correct gauge if necessary.

*With Light Blue, CO 14 sts and divide onto 4 dpn: 4 + 3 + 4
+ 3. Join to work in the round. Work following the Basic
Pattern on page 22 and the chart on this page.*

Place a marker on the first stitch of the tail to make it
easier to begin the embroidery motifs after the bird has
been knitted and filled.

Flatten the tail and sew the end at the cast-on row, making sure that the top and bottom sides are correctly oriented. Stretch the body well and tighten any stitches that
are too loose.

Single-color birds are more flexible than birds with color
patterns, so you can shape them to your liking as you fill
them.
Block by gently steam pressing under a damp pressing
cloth. Fill the bird and sew the hole at top of head to
close.
Embroider the motifs with duplicate stitch.
Crochet the beak and sew on the eyes. Our bird has a
purple beak and blue eyes.

DECORATING TIP: This old three-tier serving dish is used as a table decoration.
Embellish it with fruit, flowers, and birds.

CHARACTERISTICS: *This pink bird was knitted following the Basic Pattern on page 22 and then embroidered on the back and top of the rump with dark blue, purple, gray, green, and yellow.*

ROSITA

MATERIALS

Yarn: CYCA #3 (DK weight) Schachenmayr Merino Extrafine 120 DK, 100% wool (131 yd/120 m / 50 g)
Colors: Pink 00137, Purple 00147, Dark Blue 00153, Gray 00190, Yellow 00120, Green 00174
Needles: U.S. size 0-2.5 / 2-3 mm, set of 5 dpn
Gauge: 30 sts and 40 rnds in 4 x 4 in / 10 x 10 cm.
Adjust needle size to obtain correct gauge if necessary.

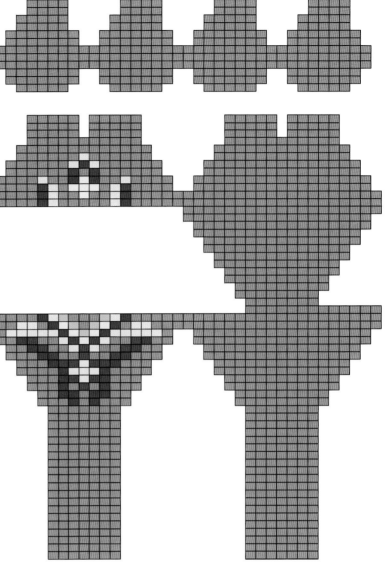

With Pink, CO 14 sts and divide onto 4 dpn: 4 + 3 + 4 + 3. Join to work in the round. Work following the Basic Pattern on page 22 and the chart on this page.

Place a marker on the first stitch of the top rump to make it easier to begin the embroidery motifs after the bird has been knitted and filled.

Flatten the tail and sew the end at the cast-on row, making sure that the top and bottom sides are correctly oriented. Stretch the body well and tighten any stitches that are too loose.

Single-color birds are more flexible than birds with color patterns, so you can shape them to your liking as you fill them.

Block by gently steam pressing under a damp pressing cloth. Fill the bird and sew the hole at top of head to close.

Embroider the motifs with duplicate stitch.

Crochet the beak and sew on the eyes. Our bird has a blue beak and blue eyes.

When decorating the birds with duplicate stitch, there are almost no limits to how many colors you can use. These single-color birds don't have any pattern strands to get twisted or tangled up in. This is a great project for using up small amounts of leftover yarn, the ones that are too nice to just toss out. Now you can use them and have a good conscience after having them lie around for many years.

CHARACTERISTICS: A green bird knitted following the Basic Pattern on page 22 and then embroidered with dark pink, burgundy, yellow, and purple.

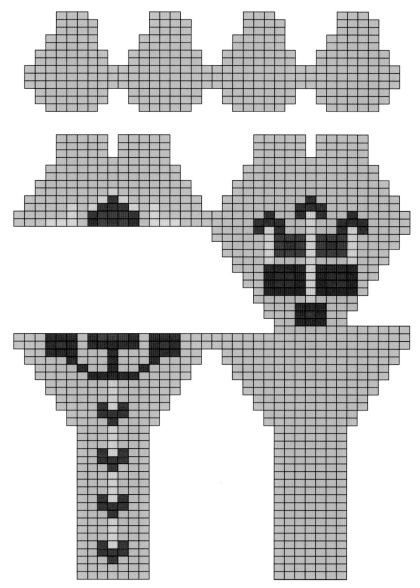

LOLA

MATERIALS

Yarn: CYCA #3 (DK weight) Schachenmayr Merino Extrafine 120 DK, 100% wool (131 yd/120 m / 50 g)
Colors: Green 00174, Burgundy 00132, Yellow 00121, Dark Pink 00138, Purple 00147
Needles: U.S. size 0-2.5 / 2-3 mm, set of 5 dpn
Gauge: 30 sts and 40 rnds in 4 x 4 in / 10 x 10 cm.
Adjust needle size to obtain correct gauge if necessary.

With Green, CO 14 sts and divide onto 4 dpn: 4 + 3 + 4 + 3. Join to work in the round. Work following the Basic Pattern on page 22 and the chart on this page.

Place markers on the first stitch of the tail and first stitch of the breast to make it easier to begin the embroidery motifs after the bird has been knitted and filled.

Flatten the tail and sew the end at the cast-on row, making sure that the top and bottom sides are correctly ori-

ented. Stretch the body well and tighten any stitches that are too loose.

Single-color birds are more flexible than birds with color patterns, so you can shape them to your liking as you fill them.

Block by gently steam pressing under a damp pressing cloth. Fill the bird and sew the hole at top of head to close.

Embroider the motifs with duplicate stitch.

Crochet the beak and sew on the eyes. Our bird has a red beak and blue eyes.

CHARACTERISTICS: Our burgundy-colored bird was knitted following the Basic Pattern on page 22 and embroidered with white and powder pink over the back, top rump, and tail.

CARMEN

MATERIALS

Yarn: CYCA #3 (DK weight) Schachenmayr Merino
Extrafine 120 DK, 100% wool (131 yd/120 m / 50 g)
Colors: Burgundy 00132, White 00101, Powder Pink
00135 + small amount of Red for beak
Needles: U.S. size 0-2.5 / 2-3 mm, set of 5 dpn
Gauge: 30 sts and 40 rnds in 4 x 4 in / 10 x 10 cm.
Adjust needle size to obtain correct gauge if necessary.

*With Burgundy, CO 14 sts and divide onto 4 dpn: 4 + 3 + 4
+ 3. Join to work in the round. Work following the Basic
Pattern on page 22 and the chart on this page.*

Place a marker on the first stitch of the tail to make it
easier to begin the embroidery motifs after the bird has
been knitted and filled.

Flatten the tail and sew the end at the cast-on row,
making sure that the top and bottom sides are correctly
oriented. Stretch the body well and tighten any stitches
that are too loose.

Single-color birds are more flexible than birds with
color patterns, so you can shape them to your liking
as you fill them.
Block by gently steam pressing under a damp pressing cloth. Fill the bird and sew the hole at top of
head to close.
Embroider the motifs with duplicate stitch.
Crochet the beak and sew on the eyes. Our bird has
a red beak and red eyes.

Chapter 6

GARDEN BIRDS

Knitted birds with patterns inspired by actual birds. You'll recognize some at first glance but we've also taken some liberties. We've changed colors on some and adjusted the patterning to fit the stitch count and limited size. We also tried to make the birds as easy as possible.

This is one of the first of the southern migrants who come back to our garden when spring arrives. It hops about from one spot to another, shakes its head, and listens. It is easy to knit and the yellow beak is so striking against the dark body.

BLACKBIRD Turdus Merula

MATERIALS

Yarn: CYCA #3 (DK weight) Schachenmayr Merino
Extrafine 120 DK, 100% wool (131 yd/120 m / 50 g)
Colors: Black 00199 and Yellow 00121
Needles: U.S. size 0-2.5 / 2-3 mm, set of 5 dpn
Gauge: 30 sts and 40 rnds in 4 x 4 in / 10 x 10 cm.
Adjust needle size to obtain correct gauge if necessary.

With Black, CO 14 sts and divide onto 4 dpn: 4 + 3 + 4 +
3. Join to work in the round. Work following the Basic
Pattern on page 22.

Flatten the tail and sew the end at the cast-on
row, making sure that the top and bottom sides are
correctly oriented. Stretch the body well and tighten
any stitches that are too loose.

Single-color birds are more flexible than birds with
color patterns, so you can shape them to your liking
as you fill them.

Block by gently steam pressing under a damp pressing
cloth. Fill the bird and sew the hole at top of head
to close.

Crochet the yellow beak and sew on the yellow eyes.

KNITTING TIP: Brighten up your window sill. With a grill skewer in its stomach. the wagtail can enhance a pot of geraniums with its companion titmouse.

TITMOUSE: A faithful guest at the bird feeder or hanging upside down on the lard ball under the veranda roof.

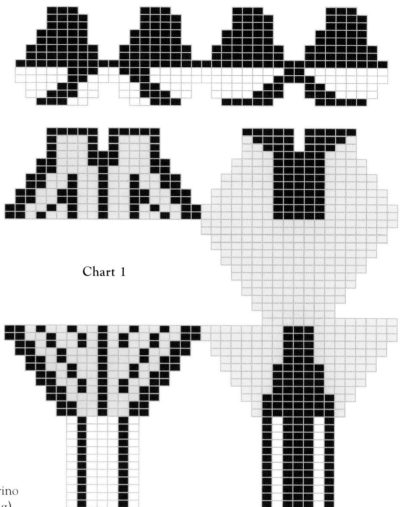

Chart 1

TITMOUSE Parus Major

MATERIALS

Yarn: CYCA #3 (DK weight) Schachenmayr Merino Extrafine 120 DK, 100% wool (131 yd/120 m / 50 g)
Colors: Black 00199, White 00102, Yellow 00120, Gray 00192
Needles: U.S. size 0-2.5 / 2-3 mm, set of 5 dpn
Gauge: 30 sts and 40 rnds in 4 x 4 in / 10 x 10 cm.
Adjust needle size to obtain correct gauge if necessary.

With Black, CO 14 sts and divide onto 4 dpn: 4 + 3 + 4 + 3. Join to work in the round.

TAIL

Work 13 rnds following the chart.
Work following the Basic Pattern on page 22.

RUMP

This pattern varies from the Basic Pattern on Rnds 1 and 3:
Rnd 1: K1, inc 1, k4, inc 1, k3, inc 1, k4, inc 1, k2.
Rnd 2: K18.
Rnd 3: K1, Inc 1, k7, inc 1, k2, inc 1, k7, inc 1, k1.
Rnd 4: K22.
Rnd 5: (K1, inc 1, k9, inc 1, k1) 2 times.

Rnd 6: K26.
Rnd 7: (K1, inc 1, k11, inc 1, k1) 2 times.
Rnd 8: K30.
Rnd 9: (K1, inc 1, k13, inc 1, k1) 2 times.
Rnd 10: K34.
Rnd 11: (K1, inc 1, k15, inc 1, k1) 2 times.
Rnd 12: K38.

Now continue the rest of the body following the Basic Pattern on page 22.

Stretch the body well and tighten any stitches that are too loose, especially where you worked back and forth.

HEAD

The instructions vary from the Basic Pattern on Rnds 2 and 4 for the head because we wanted clear stitches

75

The pattern continues on next page

Chart II
(Embroider the Gray on the back)

at the back of the head, to make it easier to embroider with duplicate stitch after the bird has been knitted and blocked.

Rnd 1: K20.
Rnd 2: Over Needles 1 and 2: (K1, inc 1, k3, inc 1, k1) 2 times.
Over Ndls 3 and 4: (K1, inc 1, k1, inc 1, k5, inc 1, k1, inc 1, k2).
Rnd 3: K28.
Rnd 4: Ndls 1 and 2: (K1, inc 1, k5, inc 1, k1) 2 times; Ndls 3 and 4: K1, inc 1, k3, inc 1, k5, inc 1, k4, inc 1, k1.
Rnd 5: K36.
Rnd 6: K36.
Rnd 7: (K1, k2tog, k3, k2tog, k1) around.
Rnd 8: K28.
Rnd 9: (K1, k2tog, k1, k2tog, k1) around.

Rnd 10: K20.
Rnd 11: (K1, k2tog, k2) around.
Rnd 12: K16.
Rnd 13: (K1, k2tog, k1) around.

Cut yarn and draw end through rem 12 sts.
Flatten the tail and sew the end at the cast-on row, making sure that the top and bottom sides are correctly oriented. Stretch the body well and tighten any stitches that are too loose.
Block by gently steam pressing under a damp pressing cloth. Fill the bird and sew the hole at top of head to close.
Crochet the beak and sew on the eyes. Our bird has a gray beak and dark blue eyes.
Embroider the back with duplicate stitch in Gray.

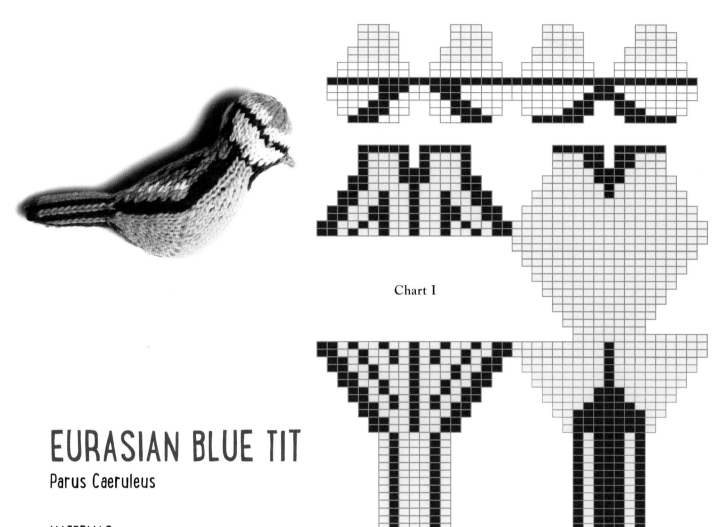

Chart I

EURASIAN BLUE TIT

Parus Caeruleus

MATERIALS

Yarn: CYCA #3 (DK weight) Schachenmayr Merino Extrafine 120 DK, 100% wool (131 yd/120 m / 50 g)
Colors: Black 00199, White 00102, Yellow 00120, Blue 00165, Green 00174
Needles: U.S. size 0-2.5 / 2-3 mm, set of 5 dpn
Gauge: 30 sts and 40 rnds in 4 x 4 in / 10 x 10 cm.
Adjust needle size to obtain correct gauge if necessary.

With Black, CO 14 sts and divide onto 4 dpn: 4 + 3 + 4 + 3. Join to work in the round.

TAIL

Work 13 rnds following the chart.
Work following the Basic Pattern on page 22.

RUMP

This pattern varies from the Basic Pattern on Rnds 1 and 3:
Rnd 1: K1, inc 1, k4, inc 1, k3, inc 1, k4, inc 1, k2.

Rnd 2: K18.
Rnd 3: Inc 1, k8, inc 1, k2, inc 1, k7, inc 1, k1.
Rnd 4: K22.
Rnd 5: (K1, inc 1, k9, inc 1, k1) 2 times.
Rnd 6: K26.
Rnd 7: (K1, inc 1, k11, inc 1, k1) 2 times.
Rnd 8: K30.
Rnd 9: (K1, inc 1, k13, inc 1, k1) 2 times.
Rnd 10: K34.
Rnd 11: (K1, inc 1, k15, inc 1, k1) 2 times.
Rnd 12: K38.

Now continue the rest of the body following the Basic Pattern on page 22.

The pattern continues on page 79

One morning, while we sat and knitted and listened to the radio, a nature program came on. They talked about how colorful the Eurasian blue tit is and how people really hadn't realized that they had a small exotic creature at their bird feeders. Of course, we had to take a closer look at the blue tit and that's how this one came into the world.

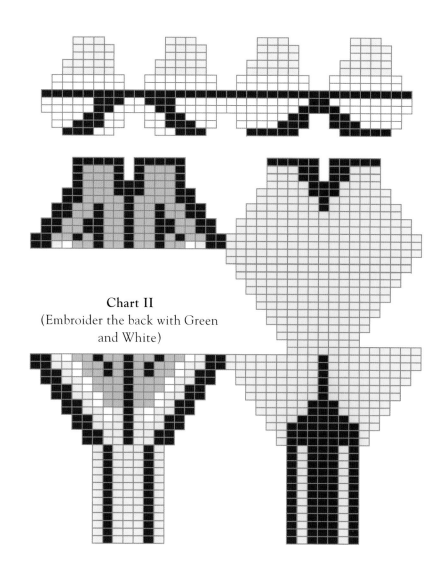

Chart II
(Embroider the back with Green
and White)

HEAD

The instructions vary from the Basic Pattern on Rnds 2 and 4 for the head because we wanted clear stitches at the back of the head, to make it easier to embroider with duplicate stitch after the bird has been knitted and blocked.

Rnd 1: K20.
Rnd 2: Needles 1 and 2: (K1, inc 1, k3, inc 1, k1) 2 times. Over Ndls 3 and 4, work: (K1, inc 1, k1, inc 1, k5, inc 1, k1, inc 1, k2).
Rnd 3: K28.
Rnd 4: Ndls 1 and 2: (K1, inc 1, k5, inc 1, k1) 2 times; Ndls 3 and 4: K1, inc 1, k3, inc 1, k5, inc 1, k4, inc 1, k1.
Rnd 5: K36.
Rnd 6: K36.
Rnd 7: (K1, k2tog, k3, k2tog, k1) around.
Rnd 8: K28.

Rnd 9: (K1, k2tog, k1, k2tog, k1) around.
Rnd 10: K20.
Rnd 11: (K1, k2tog, k2) around.
Rnd 12: K16.
Rnd 13: (K1, k2tog, k1) around.

Cut yarn and draw end through rem 12 sts.
Flatten the tail and sew the end at the cast-on row, making sure that the top and bottom sides are correctly oriented. Stretch the body well and tighten any stitches that are too loose.
Block by gently steam pressing under a damp pressing cloth. Fill the bird and sew the hole at top of head to close Crochet the beak and sew on the eyes. Our bird has a blue beak and blue eyes.
Embroider the motifs on the back with duplicate stitch in Green and White following chart II.

TEA COZY WITH BLUE TIT

MATERIALS

Yarn: CYCA #3 (DK weight) Schachenmayr Merino Extrafine 120 DK, 100% wool (131 yd/120 m / 50 g)
Colors: Blue 00165, Yellow 00120, White 00102, Black 00199, one 50 g ball each color
Needles: U.S. sizes 2.5 and 4 / 3 and 3.5 mm, set of 5 dpn and 16 in / 40 cm circulars
Gauge: 22 sts and 30 rnds on larger needles in 4 x 4 in / 10 x 10 cm. Adjust needle sizes to obtain correct gauge if necessary.

With Blue and short circular U.S. size 2.5 / 3 mm, CO 96 sts. Join, being careful not to twist cast-on row; place marker for beginning of rnd.
Work 15 rnds in k2, p2 ribbing.
Change to larger size circular and knit 1 rnd, increasing 2 sts evenly spaced around = 98 sts.
Now work each side of the cozy separately. Rows are worked back and forth on the circular, with the other half of the stitches (= 49 sts) resting on the same circular or on a holder.
Work 49 sts following the bottom chart on page 81; begin each row of the chart with sl 1, k3, and end with k4 (= garter stitch vertical panel).
When beginning a row with a slip st, it is important to make sure that the yarn at the beginning of the row doesn't tighten the slipped stitch. The edge stitches should lie smoothly, one above the other, along the edge. All of the edge stitches should be "open." One method for making an open chain edge is to begin each row with sl 1 knitwise with yarn in back and end each row with p1.

Chart: Work back and forth in knit and purl stockinette / stocking stitch rows. After completing the 17 rows of lower chart for one side, work the other side of the cozy the same way.

Now join the two pieces on Row 18 (1ˢᵗ row of top chart): Sl 1, k3, p44, purl the last st of Piece 1 together with the first st of Piece 2. The opening for the spout is complete; continue with p44, k4.

Work back and forth over 97 sts following the chart: Begin the row with sl 1, k98.
Work 7 more rows in stockinette / stocking stitch, following the chart. Begin each row of the chart with sl 1, k3, and end with k4.

Rnd 8: Now work in the round again—begin with k1 and then sl the last st of Row 7 over the knit st. The opening for the handle is complete.

Continue following the chart:
Rnd 9: (K2tog, k6) around.
Rnd 10: K84.
Move sts to dpn on the next rnd, dividing them evenly onto 4 larger dpn.
Rnd 11: (K2tog, k5) around.
Rnd 12: K72.
Rnd 13: (K2tog, k4) around.
Rnd 14: K60.
Rnd 15: (K2tog, k3) around.
Rnd 16: K48.
Rnd 17: (K2tog, k2) around.
Rnd 18: K36.
Rnd 19: (K2tog, k1) around.
Rnd 20: K24.
Change to smaller dpn and finish the cozy with 15 rnds of k2, p2 ribbing.
BO knitwise.
Weave in all ends neatly on WS and tighten any loose strands, especially in the section worked back and forth.
Gently steam press the cozy under a damp pressing cloth.
Knit a bird.

For this cozy, we sewed a Eurasian blue tit on top. So that the bird won't roll off, insert a ring of cardboard under the top ribbing and then fold the ribbing over it. Baste the bird to the top.
If you want a smaller bird on the tea cozy, make one with a smaller needle size.

A tea setting inspired by Alice in Wonderland.
We placed a bird on the hat and knitted a tea
cozy with the colors of a blue tit.

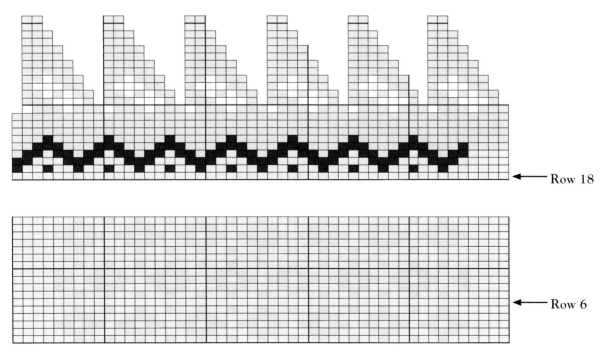

← Row 18

← Row 6

81

Every spring they return to our garden. For many years, they nested on a roost in our old outhouse. Eventually, we had to seal off all the openings because the swallows flew in. Now they hang out at another place in the garden but we don't know exactly where. We also know that one of them comes back every year because it has only one leg.

WHITE WAGTAIL

Motacilla Alba

MATERIALS

Yarn: CYCA #3 (DK weight) Schachenmayr
Merino Extrafine 120 DK, 100% wool (131 yd/
120 m / 50 g)
Colors: Black 00199, White 00101, Gray 00192
Needles: U.S. size 0-2.5 / 2-3 mm, set of 5 dpn
Gauge: 30 sts and 40 rnds in 4 x 4 in / 10 x
10 cm. Adjust needle size to obtain correct gauge
if necessary.

*With Black, CO 14 sts and divide onto 4 dpn: 4 + 3 + 4 + 3.
Join to work in the round.*

TAIL

Work 27 rnds following the Basic Pattern on
page 22 and the chart here.

RUMP

This pattern varies from the Basic Pattern on Rnd 1:
Rnd 1: K1, inc 1, k4, inc 1, k3, inc 1, k5, inc 1, k1.
Rnd 2: K18.
Rnd 3: (K1, inc 1, k7, inc 1, k1) 2 times.
Rnd 4: K22.
Rnd 5: (K1, inc 1, k9, inc 1, k1) 2 times.
Rnd 6: K26.
Rnd 7: (K1, inc 1, k11, inc 1, k1) 2 times.
Rnd 8: K30.
Rnd 9: (K1, inc 1, k13, inc 1, k1) 2 times.
Rnd 10: K34.
Rnd 11: (K1, inc 1, k15, inc 1, k1) 2 times.
Rnd 12: K38.

Now continue the rest of the body following the Basic
Pattern on page 22.

HEAD

**The instructions vary from the Basic Pattern on Rnds
2 and 4 for the head because we wanted clear stitches
at the back of the head.**

Rnd 1: K20.
Rnd 2: Ndls 1 and 2: (K1, inc 1, k3, inc 1, k1) 2 times.
Ndls 3 and 4: (K1, inc 1, k1, inc 1, k5, inc 1, k1, inc 1,
k2).
Rnd 3: K28.
Rnd 4: Ndls 1 and 2: (K1, inc 1, k5, inc 1, k1) 2 times;
Ndls 3 and 4: K1, inc 1, k3, inc 1, k5, inc 1, k4, inc 1, k1.

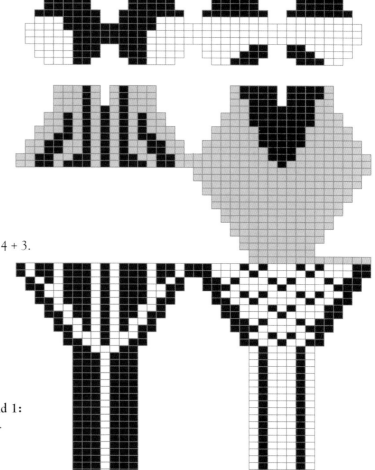

Rnd 5: K36.
Rnd 6: K36.
Rnd 7: (K1, k2tog, k3, k2tog, k1) around.
Rnd 8: K28.
Rnd 9: (K1, k2tog, k1, k2tog, k1) around.
Rnd 10: K20.
Rnd 11: (K1, k2tog, k2) around.
Rnd 12: K16.
Rnd 13: (K1, k2tog, k1) around.

Cut yarn and draw end through rem 12 sts.
Flatten the tail and sew the end at the cast-on row,
making sure that the top and bottom sides are correctly
oriented. Stretch the body well and tighten any stitches
that are too loose.
Block by gently steam pressing under a damp pressing cloth. Fill the bird and sew the hole at top of head
to close.
Crochet the beak and sew on the eyes. Our bird has a
black beak and black eyes.

KNITTING TIP: Place a barn swallow on the roof of an old birdhouse and use to decorate your window.

A few years ago, for a few weeks, we had the company of a little swallow on our veranda. It rained quite a bit that spring so it found a very peaceful spot under the roof. Perhaps it liked to have a little company in the evenings. It sat and half-slept all evening and flew out every morning when we took our dog Freja out.

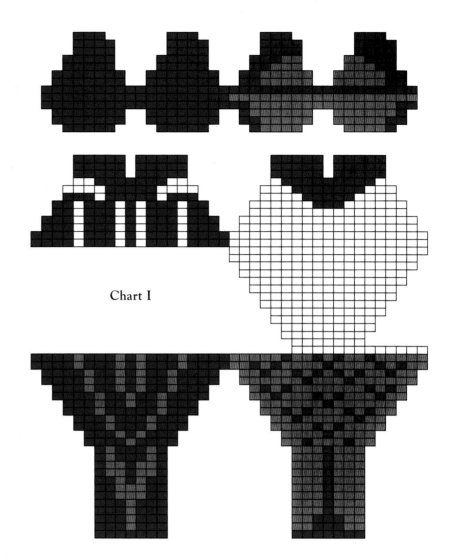

Chart I

BARN SWALLOW
Hirundo Rustica

MATERIALS

Yarn: CYCA #3 (DK weight) Schachenmayr Merino Extrafine 120 DK, 100% wool (131 yd/120 m / 50 g)
Colors: Dark blue 00150, Orange 00125, White 00101, Blue 00151
Needles: U.S. size 0-2.5 / 2-3 mm, set of 5 dpn
Gauge: 30 sts and 40 rnds in 4 x 4 in / 10 x 10 cm.
Adjust needle size to obtain correct gauge if necessary.

Begin by making the split swallow tail. With Dark Blue, CO 4 sts. *K4 and then move the sts back to front of needle. Pull working yarn behind needle and rep from * until you have a total of 20 rows.
Rnd 21: K1, inc 1, k2, inc 1, k1. Divide sts over 3 needles with 2 sts on each needle.
Rnds 22-36: Knit 15 rnds with 6 sts.
Rnd 37: K1, inc 1, k4, inc 1, k1.
Rnds 38-44: Knit 8 rnds with 8 sts.
Rnd 45: K1, inc 1, k6, inc 1, k1.
Rnds 46-48: K10 each round.
Rnd 49: BO 2 sts, k6 (including last st of bind-off), BO 2 sts.

Make another tail section the same way.

Now knit the two tail feather sections together as follows: Divide the sts over 4 dpn with 3 sts on each needle.
Begin between the 6 sts on the outer side of the tail, opposite the side with the increases. Make sure that the 4 bound-off sts of each tail section align with each other when you knit them together.
Rnds 50-52: K12.
Rnd 53: K3, inc 1, k6, inc 1, k3.

Now continue, following the Basic Pattern on page 22 and the chart on this page.

85

The pattern continues on the next page

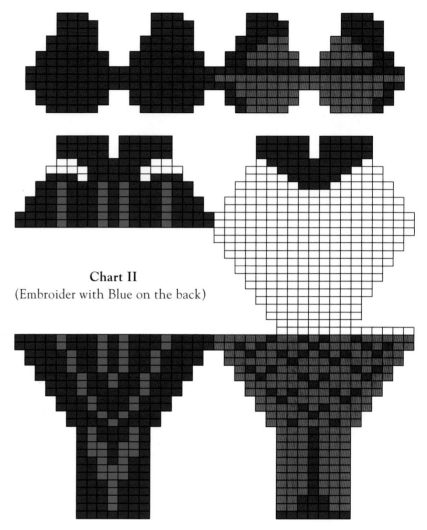

Chart II
(Embroider with Blue on the back)

Make sure the stitches are divided onto 4 dpn: 4 + 3 + 4 + 3.
Knit 12 rnds following the chart.

Cut yarn and draw end through rem 12 sts.
Weave in all ends neatly to WS. Seam the bound-off sts between the tail sections.
Stretch the body well and tighten any stitches that are too loose.
Block by gently steam pressing under a damp pressing cloth. Fill the bird and sew the hole at top of head to close.
Place the orange eyes in the blue stripe over the face and crochet a dark blue beak.
Embroider the motifs on the back with duplicate stitch in Blue, following the chart.

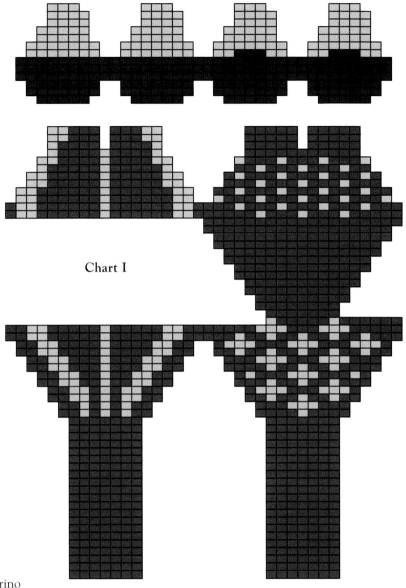

Chart I

REDTAIL
Phoenicurus Phoenicurus

MATERIALS

Yarn: CYCA #3 (DK weight) Schachenmayr Merino Extrafine 120 DK, 100% wool (131 yd/120 m / 50 g)
Colors: Red 00131, Gray 00192, Burgundy 00133, Black 00199
Needles: U.S. size 0-2.5 / 2-3 mm, set of 5 dpn
Gauge: 30 sts and 40 rnds in 4 x 4 in / 10 x 10 cm.
Adjust needle size to obtain correct gauge if necessary.

With Red, CO 14 sts and divide onto 4 dpn: 4 + 3 + 4 + 3. Join to work in the round.

TAIL

Work 21 rnds.
Continue with the body following the Basic Pattern on page 22 and the chart on this page.

Cut yarn and draw end through rem 12 sts.

Flatten the tail and sew the end at the cast-on row, making sure that the top and bottom sides are correctly oriented. Stretch the body well and tighten any stitches that are too loose.
Block by gently steam pressing under a damp pressing cloth. Fill the bird and sew the hole at top of head to close.
Crochet the beak and sew on the eyes. This bird has a gray beak and blue eyes.

87

The pattern continues on page 89

With the shade of red we used for our redtail, this bird can also come out for Christmas.

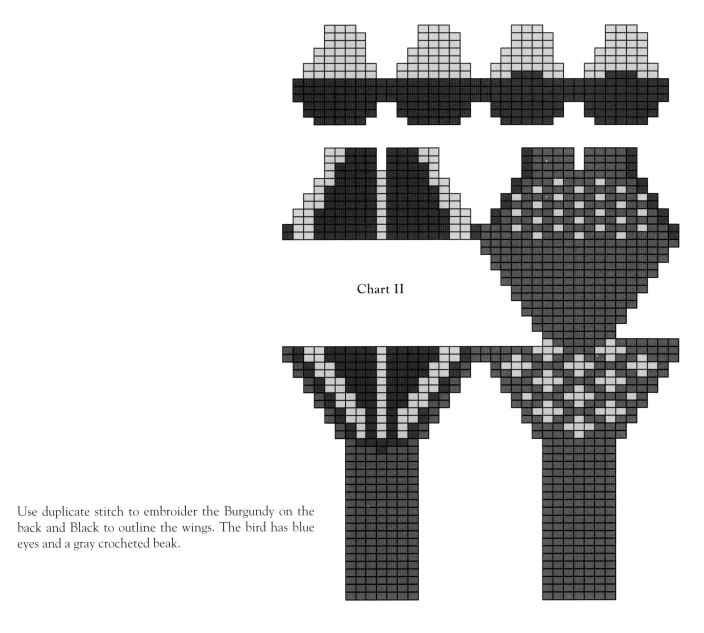

Chart II

Use duplicate stitch to embroider the Burgundy on the back and Black to outline the wings. The bird has blue eyes and a gray crocheted beak.

A redtail paired with a bullfinch makes a lovely Christmas decoration.

The bullfinch is knitted in three colors following the Basic Pattern on page 22. There's no stranded patterning and no embroidery. We decided to make this bird as easy as possible. With the single-color head, it can look out in any direction no matter where you place the beak and eyes.

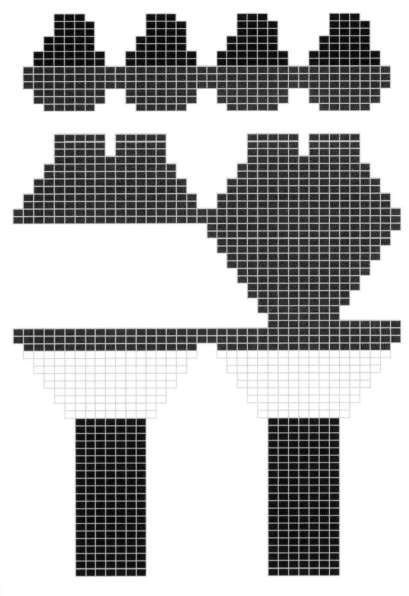

BULLFINCH Pyrrhula Pyrrhula

MATERIALS

Yarn: CYCA #3 (DK weight) Schachenmayr Merino Extrafine 120 DK, 100% wool (131 yd/120 m / 50 g)
Colors: Black 00199, White 00102, Red 00131
Needles: U.S. size 0-2.5 / 2-3 mm, set of 5 dpn
Gauge: 30 sts and 40 rnds in 4 x 4 in / 10 x 10 cm. Adjust needle size to obtain correct gauge if necessary.

With Black, CO 14 sts and divide onto 4 dpn: 4 + 3 + 4 + 3. Join to work in the round.

Work following the Basic Pattern on page 22 and the chart on this page.

Flatten the tail and sew the end at the cast-on row, making sure that the top and bottom sides are correctly oriented. Stretch the body well and tighten any stitches that are too loose. Birds without any stranded patterning are more flexible than those knitted in pattern so you can shape them as you like when you fill them.
Block by gently steam pressing under a damp pressing cloth. Fill the bird and sew the hole at top of head to close.
Crochet the beak and sew on the eyes. This bird has a black beak and dark gray eyes.

91

In the summer of 2015, a new guest popped up in our garden. Its appearance and behavior matched the description of a robin, although its breast was less red than shown on Christmas cards. So, we made two versions—one with an orange breast and one with red, just to be sure. The bird wasn't especially shy. It came out of the bushes and perennials and stared at us when we sat in the garden. We hope it has come to stay. It's a really nice guest to have in the garden—but if that doesn't happen, we can put out one that we knitted ourselves.

Chart I

Chart II
(Embroider the Gray on the back)

ROBIN Erithacus Rubecula

MATERIALS

Yarn: CYCA #3 (DK weight) Schachenmayr Merino Extrafine 120 DK, 100% wool (131 yd/120 m / 50 g)
Colors: White 00101, Black 00199, Orange 00125, Gray 00191
Needles: U.S. size 0-2.5 / 2-3 mm, set of 5 dpn
Gauge: 30 sts and 40 rnds in 4 x 4 in / 10 x 10 cm.
Adjust needle size to obtain correct gauge if necessary.

With White, CO 14 sts and divide onto 4 dpn: 4 + 3 + 4 + 3. Join to work in the round.

TAIL

Work following the Basic Pattern on page 22 and Chart I on this page.

Cut yarn and draw end through rem 12 sts.
Flatten the tail and sew the end at the cast-on row, making sure that the top and bottom sides are correctly oriented. Stretch the body well and tighten any stitches that are too loose.
Block by gently steam pressing under a damp pressing cloth. Fill the bird and sew the hole at top of head to close.
Crochet the beak and sew on the eyes. This bird has a black beak and black eyes.
With Gray, following Chart II, embroider in duplicate stitch between the two black stitches on the back and up to the last black row at the neck.

TEA COZY WITH A ROBIN

MATERIALS

Yarn: CYCA #3 (DK weight) Schachenmayr Merino Extrafine 120 DK, 100% wool (131 yd/120 m / 50 g)
Colors: Dark Green 00172, Orange 00125, White 00101, Blue 00151, one ball of each
Needles: U.S. sizes 2.5 and 4 / 3 and 3.5 mm, 16 in / 40 cm circulars and set of 5 dpn
Gauge: 22 sts and 30 rnds in 4 x 4 in / 10 x 10 cm. Adjust needle size to obtain correct gauge if necessary.

We knitted this tea cozy with the colors of the robin but added a little blue to brighten up the cozy. To match, the robin on top has blue over its back as well as a blue beak and blue eyes.

The pattern for the tea cozy is on pages 80-81.

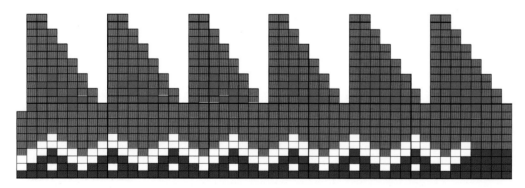

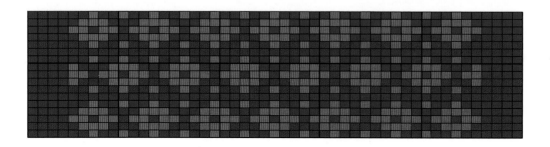

This was one of the first birds we knitted. We just had to try imitating the pretty pattern we saw on the underside of the tail.

Chart I

LONG-TAILED TIT

Aegithalos Caudatus

MATERIALS

Yarn: CYCA #3 (DK weight) Schachenmayr Merino Extrafine 120 DK, 100% wool (131 yd/120 m / 50 g)
Colors: White 00101, Black 00199, Coral 00134
Needles: U.S. size 0-2.5 / 2-3 mm, set of 5 dpn
Gauge: 30 sts and 40 rnds in 4 x 4 in / 10 x 10 cm.
Adjust needle size to obtain correct gauge if necessary.

With White, CO 14 sts and divide onto 4 dpn: 4 + 3 + 4 + 3. Join to work in the round.

NOTE: The tail has long jumps in the pattern, so in this case the yarn being carried must be twisted around the working yarn so the tail won't pull in. On the body, the bird has patterning only on the top of the rump and the back, so you will also have to frequently twist the floats around the working yarn on the wrong side when work-

ing these sections. Remember not to twist the yarns between the stitches at the same place on each round. If the twists are stacked, they'll show through on the right side.

TAIL

Work 31 rnds following the chart on this page. Continue, following the Basic Pattern on page 22 except as follows.

The pattern continues on page 99

Dried grain stalks and gourds make fine decorations when paired with a long-tailed tit and an Ortolan bunting.

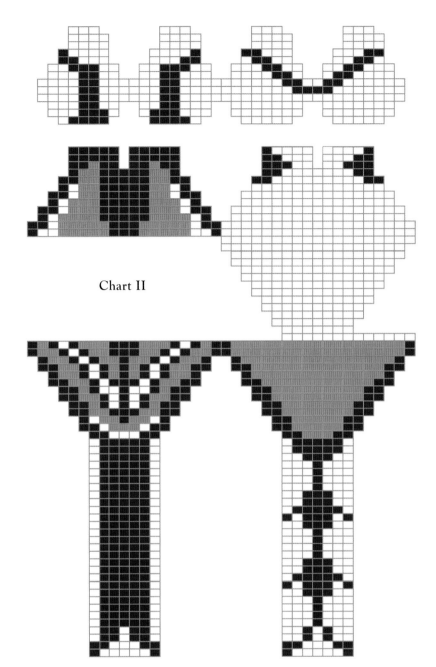

Chart II

RUMP

This pattern varies from the Basic Pattern on Rnd 1:
Rnd 1: (K1, inc 1, k4, inc 1, k2) 2 times.
Rnd 2: K18.
Rnd 3: (K1, inc 1, k7, inc 1, k1) 2 times.
Rnd 4: K22.
Rnd 5: (K1, inc 1, k9, inc 1, k1) 2 times.
Rnd 6: K26.
Rnd 7: (K1, inc 1, k11, inc 1, k1) 2 times.
Rnd 8: K30.
Rnd 9: (K1, inc 1, k13, inc 1, k1) 2 times.
Rnd 10: K34.
Rnd 11: (K1, inc 1, k15, inc 1, k1) 2 times.
Rnd 12: K38.

Now continue the rest of the body following the Basic Pattern on page 22.

Cut yarn and draw end through rem 12 sts.
Flatten the tail and sew the end at the cast-on row, making sure that the top and bottom sides are correctly oriented. Stretch the body well and tighten any stitches that are too loose.
Block by gently steam pressing under a damp pressing cloth. Fill the bird and sew the hole at top of head to close.
Using duplicate stitch, embroider the stitches on the back and top rump with White and Coral.
Crochet the beak and sew on the eyes. This bird has a black beak and blue eyes.

99

This bird was inspired by one we read about in an old bird book. It is a bird seldom seen in Norway, and we can attest to that as we've never seen any other than the ones we've knitted.

ORTOLAN BUNTING
Emberiza Hortulana

MATERIALS

Yarn: CYCA #3 (DK weight) Schachenmayr Merino Extrafine 120 DK, 100% wool (131 yd/120 m / 50 g)
Colors: White 00101, Brown 00110, Mocha 00112, Yellow 00121, Light Green 00174
Needles: U.S. size 0-2.5 / 2-3 mm, set of 5 dpn
Gauge: 30 sts and 40 rnds in 4 x 4 in / 10 x 10 cm. Adjust needle size to obtain correct gauge if necessary.

With White, CO 14 sts and divide onto 4 dpn:
4 + 3 + 4 + 3. Join to work in the round.

TAIL

Work 17 rnds following the chart on this page. Continue, following the Basic Pattern on page 22, except as noted below.

RUMP

This pattern varies from the Basic Pattern on Rnds 1 and 3:
Rnd 1: K1, inc 1, k5, inc 1, k3, inc 1, k4, inc 1, k1.
Rnd 2: K18.
Rnd 3: K1, inc 1, k7, inc 1, k1, inc 1, k8, inc 1, k1.
Rnd 4: K22.
Rnd 5: (K1, inc 1, k9, inc 1, k1) 2 times.
Rnd 6: K26.
Rnd 7: (K1, inc 1, k11, inc 1, k1) 2 times.
Rnd 8: K30.
Rnd 9: (K1, inc 1, k13, inc 1, k1) 2 times.
Rnd 10: K34.
Rnd 11: (K1, inc 1, k15, inc 1, k1) 2 times.
Rnd 12: K38.

Now continue the rest of the body following the Basic Pattern on page 22 and the chart on this page.

HEAD

The instructions for the head vary from the Basic Pattern on Rnd 11.
Rnd 1: K20.
Rnd 2: (K1, inc 1, k3, inc 1, k1) 4 times.
Rnd 3: K28.
Rnd 4: (K1, inc 1, k5, inc 1, k1) 4 times.

Rnd 5: K36.
Rnd 6: K36.
Rnd 7: (K1, k2tog, k3, k2tog, k1) 4 times.
Rnd 8: K28.
Rnd 9: (K1, k2tog, k1, k2tog, k1) 4 times.
Rnd 10: K20.
Rnd 11: (K1, k2tog, k4, k2tog, k1) 2 times.
Rnd 12: K16.
Rnd 13: (K1, k2tog, k1) around.

Cut yarn and draw end through rem 12 sts.
Flatten the tail and sew the end at the cast-on row, making sure that the top and bottom sides are correctly oriented. Stretch the body well and tighten any stitches that are too loose.
Block by gently steam pressing under a damp pressing cloth. Fill the bird and sew the hole at top of head to close.
Crochet the beak and sew on the eyes. This bird has a white beak and dark blue eyes.

MOBILE WITH BIRDS

DESIGN TIP: Make a pretty bird mobile for the children's room. Using steel wire, form a circle. The wire comes in packs already coiled in circles, which can be stretched out to a new size as desired. When the circle is the size we want, we wrap the area where the wire overlaps with masking tape to keep the circle intact. Next, we lay short lengths of super glue on the wire and wrap blue yarn around until the entire circle is covered with blue yarn. We added four doubled blue strands to hang the mobile.

These birds are knitted as for the Ortolan Bunting on page 101 with feathers glued on the sides at the transition between the stomach and the breast. We knitted the birds with the following color combinations:

BLUE BIRD: Light Blue 00152, Dark Blue 00151, Medium Blue 00165, Turquoise 00168, Gray 00190
YELLOW BIRD: White 00101, Orange 00125, Sun Yellow 00120, Yellow 00121
GREEN BIRD: Light Green 00175, Dark Green 00172, Green 00174, Apple Green 00173, Gray 00190
RED BIRD: Pink 00137, Burgundy 00133, Red 00130, Orange 00125, Powder Pink 00135
PINK BIRD: Dark Pink 00138, White 00101, Pink 00137, Powder Pink 00135

A BIRD FOR CHRISTMAS

KNITTING TIP: Knit a bird or two to give as presents to the person who has everything. Here in Norway, robins are often seen as Christmas motifs. For our pair, one has an orange breast and the other a red breast.

Bullfinches are often seen in flocks. This little flock is the result of last year's Christmas workshop.

The black-billed magpie is one of our favorite birds. In real life, they are much bigger than the other birds we've been inspired by but we knitted this one the same size as usual. It has been embellished with dark green and blue sequins.

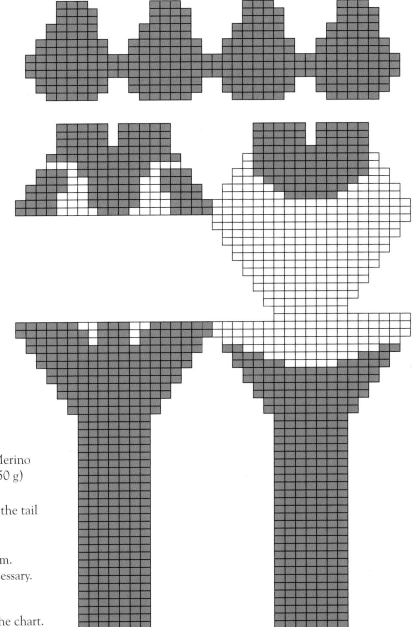

BLACK-BILLED MAGPIE

Pica Pica

MATERIALS

Yarn: CYCA #3 (DK weight) Schachenmayr Merino Extrafine 120 DK, 100% wool (131 yd/120 m / 50 g)
Colors: Black 00199, White 00101
Other Materials: Dark green-black sequins for the tail and blue sequins for the wings
Needles: U.S. size 0-2.5 / 2-3 mm, set of 5 dpn
Gauge: 30 sts and 40 rnds in 4 x 4 in / 10 x 10 cm.
Adjust needle size to obtain correct gauge if necessary.

NOTE: Use Black to knit the gray squares on the chart.

With Black, CO 14 sts and divide onto 4 dpn: 4 + 3 + 4 + 3. Join to work in the round.

TAIL

Knit 32 rnds and then continue, following the Basic Pattern on page 22 and the chart on this page.

Cut yarn and draw end through rem 12 sts.
Flatten the tail and sew the end at the cast-on row, making sure that the top and bottom sides are correctly oriented. Stretch the body well and tighten any stitches that are too loose.
Block by gently steam pressing under a damp pressing cloth. Fill the bird and sew the hole at top of head to close.

Crochet the beak and sew on the eyes. Our magpie has a black beak and blue eyes.

Sew the dark green sequins to the top of the tail and over the back. Mark the back and wings by sewing on a line of sequins. We sewed blue sequins over the back and wings. Note where the stripes of the increase and decrease lines show. Sew on the sequins between these two stripes along the side and up to the lowest white stitches centered at the base of the back. Fill in with sequins between the stripes and on the white sections at the sides.

FAMILY JEWELS

MATERIALS

Yarn: CYCA #6 (Super Bulky) Schachenmayr Wash + Filz it, 100% wool (55 yd/50 m / 50 g)
Colors: Black 00001
Other Materials: Pillow filling (about .12 oz / 3.5 g per ball)
Needles: U.S. size 8 / 5 mm, set of 5 dpn and short circular
Gauge: 11 sts and 16 rnds in 4 x 4 in / 10 x 10 cm. Adjust needle size to obtain correct gauge if necessary.

CO 12 sts and divide onto 4 dpn = 3 sts per needle. Join to knit in the round.
Rnd 1: K12.
Rnd 2: (K1, inc 1, k1, inc 1, k1) around.
Rnd 3: K20.
Rnd 4: (K1, inc 1, k3, inc 1, k1) around.
Rnd 5: K28.
Rnd 6: (K1, inc 1, k5, inc 1, k1) around.
Rnd 7: K36.
Rnd 8: (K1, inc 1, k7, inc 1, k1) around.
Rnd 9: K44.
Rnd 10: (K1, inc 1, k9, inc 1, k1) around.
Rnd 11: K52.
Rnd 12: (K1, inc 1, k11, inc 1, k1) around.
Rnd 13: K60.
Rnd 14: (K1, inc 1, k13, inc 1, k1) around.
Rnd 15: K68.
Rnd 16: (K1, inc 1, k15, inc 1, k1) around.
Rnd 17: K76.
Rnd 18: (K1, inc 1, k17, inc 1, k1) around.
Rnd 19: K84.

Rnd 20: (K1, inc 1, k19, inc 1, k1) around.
Rnd 21: K92.
Rnd 22: (K1, inc 1, k21, inc 1, k1) around.
Rnds 23-45 (= 22 rnds): K100.
Rnd 46: (K1, k2tog, k19, k2tog, k1) around.
Rnd 47: K92.
Rnd 48: (K1, k2tog, k17, k2tog, k1) around.
Rnd 49: K84.
Rnd 50: (K1, k2tog, k15, k2tog, k1) around.
Rnd 51: K76.
Rnd 52: (K1, k2tog, k13, k2tog, k1) around.
Rnd 53: K68.
Rnd 54: (K1, k2tog, k11, k2tog, k1) around.
Rnd 55: K60.
Rnd 56: (K1, k2tog, k9, k2tog, k1) around.
Rnd 57: K52.
Rnd 58: (K1, k2tog, k7, k2tog, k1) around.
Rnd 59: K44.
Rnd 60: (K1, k2tog, k5, k2tog, k1) around.
Rnd 61: K36.
Rnd 62: (K1, k2tog, k3, k2tog, k1) around.
Rnd 62: K28.
Rnd 64: (K1, k2tog, k1, k2tog, k1) around.
Rnd 65: K20.
Rnd 66: (K1, k2tog, k2) around.
Rnd 67: K16.
Rnd 68: (K1, k2tog, k1) around = 12 sts rem.

Cut yarn and draw end through rem 12 sts. Sew, closing the hole at the base and fill the ball with pillow filling. Sew the hole at the top closed. The ball, when filled, weighs .12 oz / 3.5 g before felting. Felt the ball in the washing machine with a pair of jeans.

DESIGN TIP: Knit a large black ball, fill it with pillow filling, and felt it in the washing machine. Weave a nest of twigs and set the ball in it. Now you can collect some antique jewelry, hat pins, or other old trinkets you have around. Add a magpie to guard the jewelry. Place a glass bell over it so the bird and jewelry don't get dusty. Now you've made a pretty decoration with items that would otherwise just lie in a drawer.

The finished jewelry ball and the magpie arranged under a glass bell.

Chapter 7

BIRDS IN TRADITIONAL SWEATERS

It is hard to stop knitting these birds. There are countless old motif panels you can use as inspiration. The limits placed by the Basic Pattern make the design process rather exciting because there aren't many stitches to work with. When we began knitting birds with traditional patterns, it became very freeing. You don't need to study actual birds for the sake of the patterning, but you can take the color combinations from reality.

This bird has a pattern inspired by Annichen Sibbern Bøhn's "Eskimo sweater" from 1936. We sketched the design using a picture of her sweater that we found in the book *Knitting with Icelandic Wool* (2011). In the time since the pattern for that sweater was published, round neck shaping on sweaters and cardigans has become a standard style. Our bird also has rounded shaping.

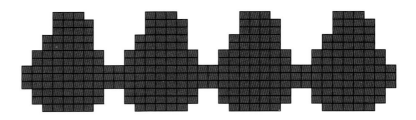

BIRD WITH AN "ESKIMO SWEATER"

MATERIALS

Yarn: CYCA #3 (DK weight) Schachenmayr Merino Extrafine 120 DK, 100% wool (131 yd/120 m / 50 g)
Colors: Gray 00190 and Dark Pink 00138; small amount Dark Blue 00153 for the beak
Needles: U.S. size 0-2.5 / 2-3 mm, set of 5 dpn
Gauge: 30 sts and 40 rnds in 4 x 4 in / 10 x 10 cm. Adjust needle size to obtain correct gauge if necessary.

With Gray, CO 14 sts and divide onto 4 dpn: 4 + 3 + 4 + 3. Join to work in the round.

TAIL

Work 21 rnds following the chart on this page. Continue, working the rump and stomach following the Basic Pattern on page 22 and the chart on this page.

BREAST

This pattern varies from the Basic Pattern for the rounded shaping:
Rnd 1: (K17, inc 1, k2) around.
Rnd 2: K40.
Rnd 3: K40.
Rnd 4: K40.
Rnd 5: K40.
Rnd 6: K3, k2tog, (k8, k2tog) 3 times; end with k5.
Rnd 7: K36.
Rnd 8: K2, k2tog, (k2tog, k5, k2tog) 3 times. End with k2tog, k3.
Rnd 9: K28. Tie or fasten off the yarn between the stomach and breast.
Rnd 10: K1, k2tog, (k2tog, k3, k2tog) 3 times; end with k2tog, k2.
Rnd 11: K20.
Rnd 12: K20.
Rnd 13: K20.

Stretch the body well and tighten any stitches that are too loose in the section worked back and forth.

Now knit the head with Dark Pink, following the Basic Pattern on page 22 and the chart on this page.

Cut yarn and draw end through rem 12 sts.
Flatten the tail and sew the end at the cast-on row, making sure that the top and bottom sides are correctly oriented.
When the head is worked with one color only, you need to be careful when you fill it so it's not too big in relation to the body.
Block by gently steam pressing under a damp pressing cloth. Fill the bird and sew the hole at top of head.
Crochet the beak and sew on the eyes. This bird has a dark blue beak and dark blue eyes.

The Carlos bird is wearing a sweater inspired by one of Carlos' favorite sweaters—an old American pullover with a round neck that he bought in Tokyo. The green stitches on the stomach are embroidered on after the bird has been knitted and filled; likewise for the burgundy red stitches forming a V at the top of the lower rump.

Chart I

BIRD WITH A CARLOS SWEATER

MATERIALS

Yarn: CYCA #3 (DK weight) Schachenmayr Merino Extrafine 120 DK, 100% wool (131 yd/120 m / 50 g)
Colors: Light Gray 00190, Burgundy 00132, Mocha 00112, Green 00172
Needles: U.S. size 0-2.5 / 2-3 mm, set of 5 dpn
Gauge: 30 sts and 40 rnds in 4 x 4 in / 10 x 10 cm. Adjust needle size to obtain correct gauge if necessary.

With Light Gray, CO 14 sts and divide onto 4 dpn: 4 + 3 + 4 + 3. Join to work in the round.

TAIL

Work 19 rnds following the chart on this page. Continue, following the Basic Pattern on page 22, except as noted below.

RUMP

This pattern varies from the Basic Pattern on Rnds 1 and 3:

Rnd 1: K1, inc 1, k5, inc 1, k1, inc 1, k6, inc 1, k1.
Rnd 2: K18.
Rnd 3: K1, inc 1, k7, inc 1, k1, inc 1, k8, inc 1, k1.
Rnd 4: K22.
Rnd 5: (K1, inc 1, k9, inc 1, k1) 2 times.
Rnd 6: K26.
Rnd 7: (K1, inc 1, k11, inc 1, k1) 2 times.
Rnd 8: K30.
Rnd 9: (K1, inc 1, k13, inc 1, k1) 2 times.
Rnd 10: K34.
Rnd 11: (K1, inc 1, k15, inc 1, k1) 2 times.
Rnd 12: K38.

113

The pattern continues on page 115

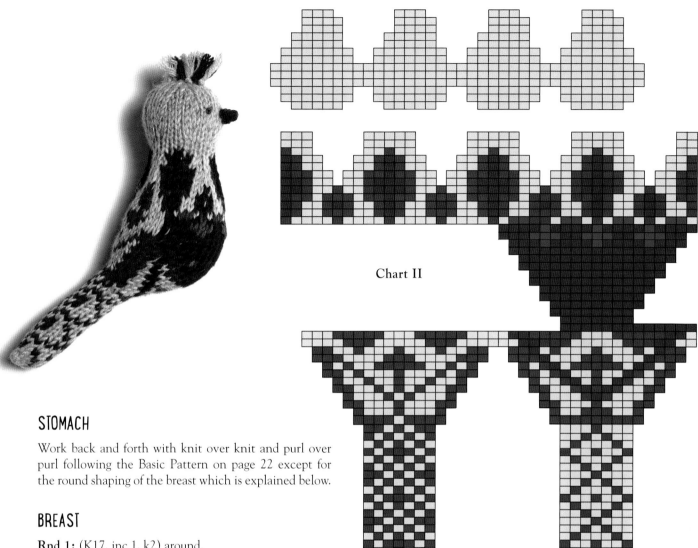

Chart II

STOMACH

Work back and forth with knit over knit and purl over purl following the Basic Pattern on page 22 except for the round shaping of the breast which is explained below.

BREAST

Rnd 1: (K17, inc 1, k2) around.
Rnd 2: K40.
Rnd 3: K40.
Rnd 4: K40.
Rnd 5: K40.
Rnd 6: K3, k2tog, (k8, k2tog) 3 times; end with k5.
Rnd 7: K36.
Rnd 8: K2, k2tog, (k2tog, k5, k2tog) 3 times. End with k2tog, k3.
Rnd 9: K28. Tie or fasten off the yarn between the stomach and breast.
Rnd 10: K1, k2tog, (k2tog, k3, k2tog) 3 times; end with k2tog, k2.
Rnd 11: K20.
Rnd 12: K20.
Rnd 13: K20.

Now continue, following the Basic Pattern on page 22.

Cut yarn and draw end through rem 12 sts.
Flatten the tail and sew the end at the cast-on row, making sure that the top and bottom sides are correctly oriented.

When the head is worked with one color only, you need to be careful when you fill it so it's not too big relative to the body.
Block by gently steam pressing under a damp pressing cloth. Fill the bird and sew the hole at top of head to close.
Embroider as indicated on chart II, working in duplicate stitch with Burgundy and Green yarn.
Crochet the beak and sew on the eyes. This bird has a brown beak and blue eyes.
If you want Carlos to have some hair, fold two strands of yarn at the center, pull them through a stitch on the head making a little loop, bring the yarn through the loop, tighten, fasten off, and trim.

115

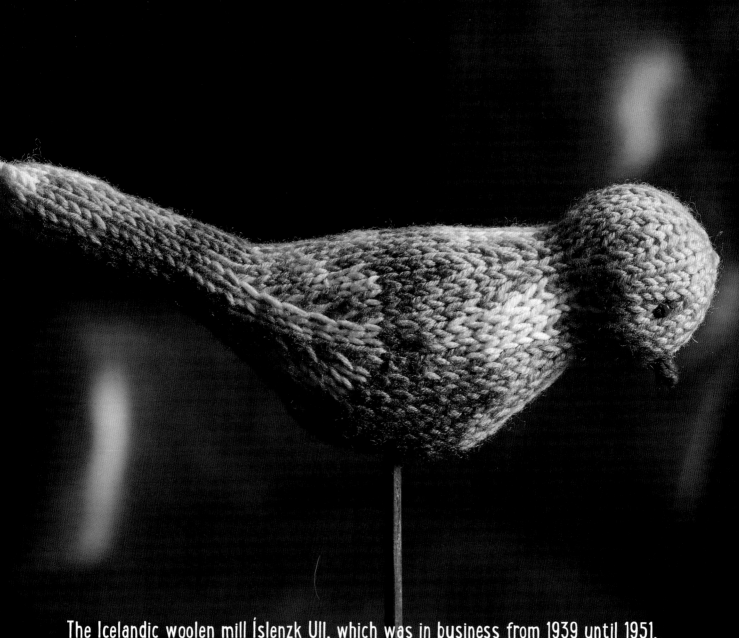

The Icelandic woolen mill Íslenzk Ull, which was in business from 1939 until 1951, published a pattern for a two-color Norwegian sweater with a rounded yoke in 1939. Following that inspiration, rounded shaping on yokes became the standard method on *lopapeysa*, or Icelandic sweaters, starting in the mid-1950s. A 1936 pattern for an Annichen Sibbern Bøhn sweater with rounded shaping was printed in the Icelandic magazine *Melkorka* in December 1956. The sweater used different colors than her original "Eskimo sweater," and was called a "Greenlandic sweater." Our Icelandic bird is knitted with three colors from the pattern inspiration we found in a book featuring people in the Icelandic landscape.

BIRD WITH AN ICELANDIC SWEATER

MATERIALS

Yarn: CYCA #3 (DK weight) Schachenmayr Merino Extrafine 120 DK, 100% wool (131 yd/ 120 m / 50 g)

Colors: Apricot 00123, Purple 00145, White 00101; small amount of Blue 00151 for beak

Needles: U.S. size 0-2.5 / 2-3 mm, set of 5 dpn

Gauge: 30 sts and 40 rnds in 4 x 4 in / 10 x 10 cm. Adjust needle size to obtain correct gauge if necessary.

With White, CO 14 sts and divide onto 4 dpn: 4 + 3 + 4 + 3. Join to work in the round.

TAIL

Work 20 rnds following the chart on this page. Continue, following the Basic Pattern on page 22 and the chart here, except as noted below.

BREAST

The breast is worked following the Basic Pattern on page 22 except for the round shaping, which is explained below.

Rnd 1: (K17, inc 1, k2) around.
Rnd 2: K40.
Rnd 3: K40.
Rnd 4: K40.
Rnd 5: K40.
Rnd 6: K3, k2tog, (k8, k2tog) 3 times; end with k5.
Rnd 7: K36.
Rnd 8: K2, k2tog, (k2tog, k5, k2tog) 3 times. End with k2tog, k3.
Rnd 9: K28. Tie or fasten off the yarn between the stomach and breast.
Rnd 10: K1, k2tog, (k2tog, k3, k2tog) 3 times; end with k2tog, k2.
Rnd 11: K20.

Rnd 12: K20.
Rnd 13: K20.

Now continue, working the head following the Basic Pattern on page 22.

Cut yarn and draw end through rem 12 sts.
Flatten the tail and sew the end at the cast-on row, making sure that the top and bottom sides are correctly oriented.
When the head is worked with one color only, you need to be careful when you fill it so it's not too big in relation to the body.
Block by gently steam pressing under a damp pressing cloth. Fill the bird and sew the hole at top of head to close.
Crochet the beak and sew on the eyes. This bird has a blue beak and blue eyes.

Another sweater inspired by one found in a used clothing shop in Tokyo. The original sweater has horizontal bands of eight-petal roses and was knitted on Shetland.

The hair: Cut two strands of yarn, twice the length you want for the hair; fold in half and bring through a stitch on the head, making a little loop. Bring the ends through the loop and fasten off.

BIRD WITH AN ARNE SWEATER

MATERIALS

Yarn: CYCA #3 (DK weight) Schachenmayr Merino Extrafine 120 DK, 100% wool (131 yd/120 m / 50 g)
Colors: Sea-Green 00166 and White 00101; small amount of Dark Blue 00153 for beak
Needles: U.S. size 0-2.5 / 2-3 mm, set of 5 dpn
Gauge: 30 sts and 40 rnds in 4 x 4 in / 10 x 10 cm. Adjust needle size to obtain correct gauge if necessary.

With White, CO 14 sts and divide onto 4 dpn: 4 + 3 + 4 + 3. Join to work in the round.

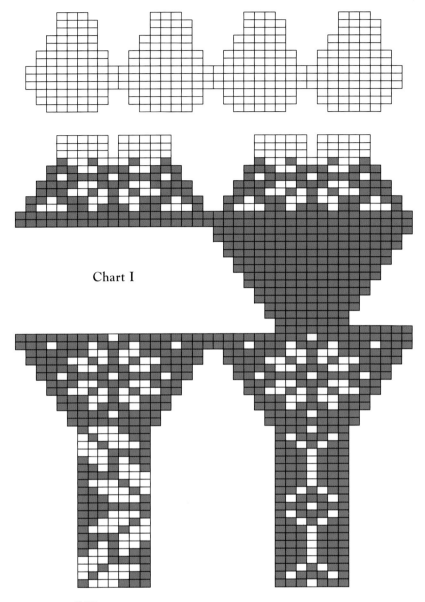

Chart I

TAIL

Work 21 rnds following Chart I on this page. Continue, following the Basic Pattern on page 22, except as noted below.

RUMP

This pattern varies from the Basic Pattern on Rnds 1 and 3:
Rnd 1: Inc 1, k6, inc 1, k2, inc 1, k5, inc 1, k1.
Rnd 2: K18.
Rnd 3: K1, inc 1, k7, inc 1, k1, inc 1, k8, inc 1, k1.
Rnd 4: K22.
Rnd 5: (K1, inc 1, k9, inc 1, k1) 2 times.
Rnd 6: K26.
Rnd 7: (K1, inc 1, k11, inc 1, k1) 2 times.
Rnd 8: K30.
Rnd 9: (K1, inc 1, k13, inc 1, k1) 2 times.

119

The pattern continues on page 120

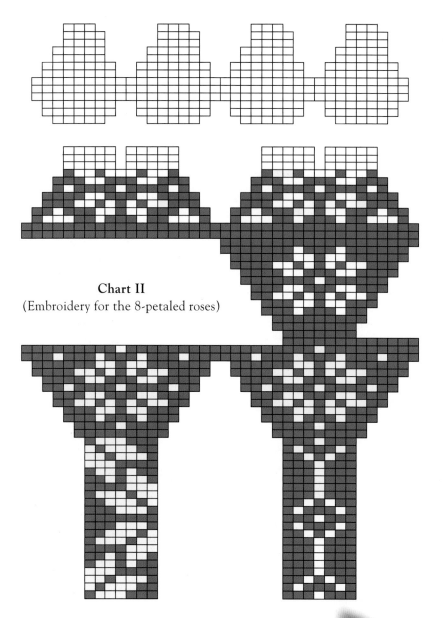

Chart II
(Embroidery for the 8-petaled roses)

Rnd 10: K34.
Rnd 11: (K1, inc 1, k15, inc 1, k1) 2 times.
Rnd 12: K38.

Continue, following Chart I and the Basic Pattern on page 22.

Cut yarn and draw end through rem 12 sts.
Flatten the tail and sew the end at the cast-on row, making sure that the top and bottom sides are correctly oriented.
Stretch the body well and tighten any stitches that are loose.
When the head is worked with one color only, you need to be careful when you fill it so it's not too big in relation to the body.
Block by gently steam pressing under a damp pressing cloth. Fill the bird and sew the hole at top of head to close.

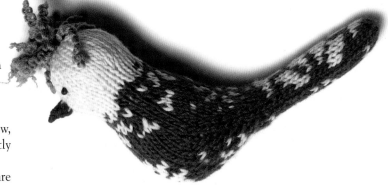

Crochet the beak and sew on the eyes. This bird has a dark blue beak and dark blue eyes.
Using duplicate stitch, embroider the eight-petaled rose on the stomach with white.

DECORATING TIP: Embellish your table with twigs, pinecones. sprigs, moss, tea candles, and birds. This is the perfect table to come home to after a long ski run or long autumn walks in the woods.

BIRD NEST TIP: Arrange traditional birds in a basket with pinecones and moss—easy and decorative.

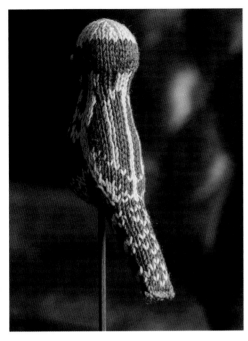

The motifs for this bird borrow elements from a Setesdal pattern. It's hard not to use these panels when the inspiration is traditional.

BIRD WITH A CROSS AND CIRCLE SWEATER

MATERIALS

Yarn: CYCA #3 (DK weight) Schachenmayr Merino Extrafine 120 DK, 100% wool (131 yd/120 m / 50 g)
Colors: Olive-Green 00171 and Lime-Green 00175
Needles: U.S. size 0-2.5 / 2-3 mm, set of 5 dpn
Gauge: 30 sts and 40 rnds in 4 x 4 in / 10 x 10 cm.
Adjust needle size to obtain correct gauge if necessary.

With Olive-Green, CO 14 sts and divide onto 4 dpn: 4 + 3 + 4 + 3. Join to work in the round.

TAIL

Work 20 rnds following the Basic Pattern on page 22 and the chart on this page.

Cut yarn and draw end through rem 12 sts.
Flatten the tail and sew the end at the cast-on row, making sure that the top and bottom sides are correctly oriented.
Stretch the body well and tighten any stitches that are loose.

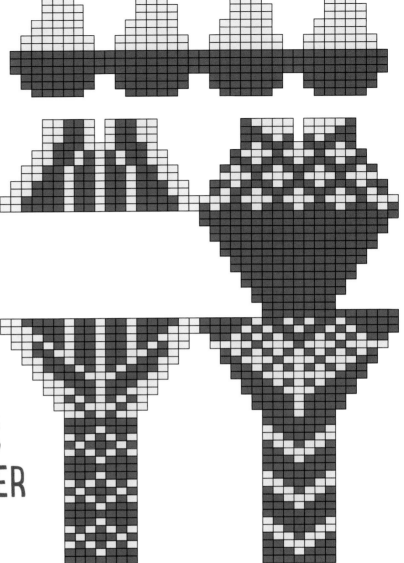

When the head is worked without any stranded patterning, you need to be careful when you fill it so it's not too big in relation to the body.
Block by gently steam pressing under a damp pressing cloth. Fill the bird and sew the hole at top of head to close.
Crochet the beak and sew on the eyes. This bird has a lime-green beak and red eyes.

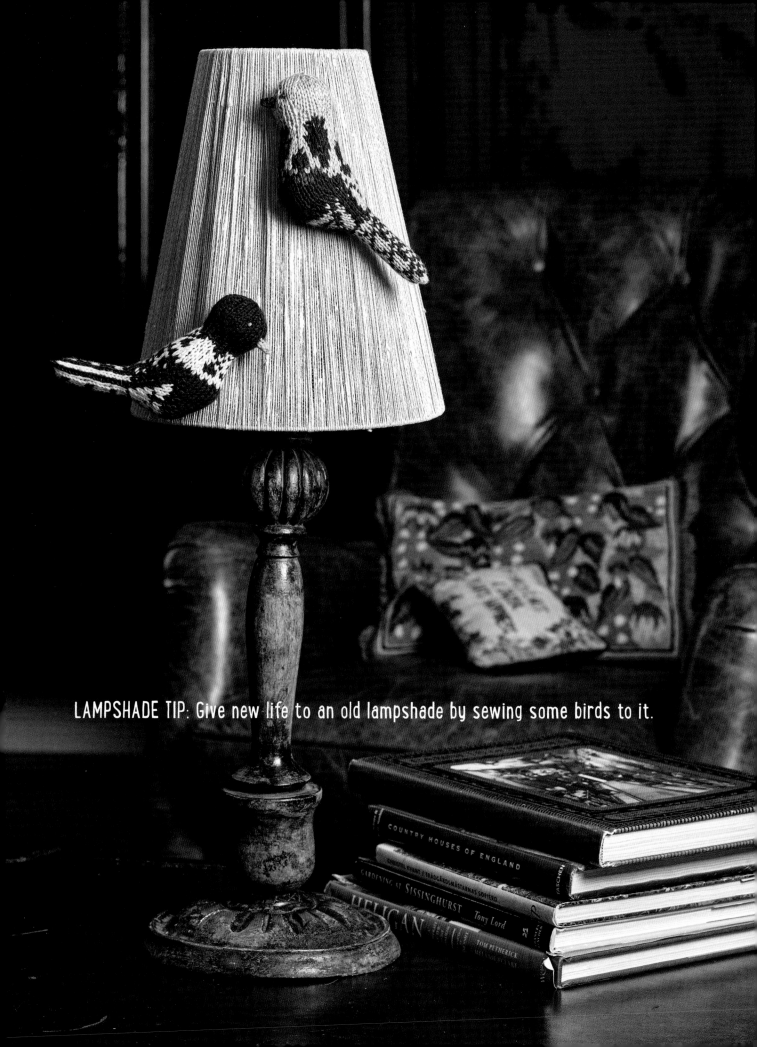

LAMPSHADE TIP: Give new life to an old lampshade by sewing some birds to it.

This bird has patterning taken from several small panels.

BIRD WITH A SWEATER OF SMALL MOTIFS

MATERIALS

Yarn: CYCA #3 (DK weight) Schachenmayr Merino Extrafine 120 DK, 100% wool (131 yd/120 m / 50 g)
Colors: White 00101 and Burgundy 00132; small amount of Yellow 00121 for beak
Needles: U.S. size 0-2.5 / 2-3 mm, set of 5 dpn
Gauge: 30 sts and 40 rnds in 4 x 4 in / 10 x 10 cm.
Adjust needle size to obtain correct gauge if necessary.

With Burgundy, CO 14 sts and divide onto 4 dpn: 4 + 3 + 4 + 3. Join to work in the round.

TAIL

Work 20 rnds following the chart on this page. Continue, following the Basic Pattern on page 22, except as noted below.

RUMP

This pattern varies from the Basic Pattern on Rnd 1:
Rnd 1: Inc 1, k6, inc 1, k2, inc 1, k4, inc 1, k2.
Rnd 2: K18.
Rnd 3: (K1, inc 1, k7, inc 1, k1) 2 times.
Rnd 4: K22.

Rnd 5: (K1, inc 1, k9, inc 1, k1) 2 times.
Rnd 6: K26.
Rnd 7: (K1, inc 1, k11, inc 1, k1) 2 times.
Rnd 8: K30.
Rnd 9: (K1, inc 1, k13, inc 1, k1) 2 times.
Rnd 10: K34.
Rnd 11: (K1, inc 1, k15, inc 1, k1) 2 times.
Rnd 12: K38.

Now continue, following the Basic Pattern on page 22.

Cut yarn and draw end through rem 12 sts.
Flatten the tail and sew the end at the cast-on row, making sure that the top and bottom sides are correctly oriented. Stretch the body well and tighten any stitches that are a bit too loose.
When the head is worked with one color only, you need to be careful when you fill it so it's not too big in relation to the body.
Block by gently steam pressing under a damp pressing cloth. Fill the bird and sew the hole at top of head to close.
Crochet the beak and sew on the eyes. This bird has a yellow beak and yellow eyes.

For this bird, we used the patterns from an old mitten. We only had one of the mittens but knew that one day we'd find a use for it. That day came when we knitted this bird.

It looks like the hunting season has started, judging by this picture. You can easily see that it was very successful this fall.

BIRD WITH A MITTEN PATTERN

MATERIALS

Yarn: CYCA #3 (DK weight) Schachenmayr Merino Extrafine 120 DK, 100% wool (131 yd/120 m / 50 g)
Colors: Olive-Green 00171 and Red 00130
Needles: U.S. size 0-2.5 / 2-3 mm, set of 5 dpn
Gauge: 30 sts and 40 rnds in 4 x 4 in / 10 x 10 cm.
Adjust needle size to obtain correct gauge if necessary.

With Red, CO 14 sts and divide onto 4 dpn: 4 + 3 + 4 + 3. Join to work in the round.

TAIL

Work 27 rnds following the chart on this page.

Continue, following the Basic Pattern on page 22.

Cut yarn and draw end through rem 12 sts.
Flatten the tail and sew the end at the cast-on row, making sure that the top and bottom sides are correctly oriented.
Stretch the body well and tighten any stitches that are loose.
Block by gently steam pressing under a damp pressing cloth. Fill the bird and sew the hole at top of head to close.
Crochet the beak and sew on the eyes. This bird has a red beak and yellow eyes.

127

Chapter 8

SPRING BIRDS

Birds inspired by spring can be used to decorate with eggs and flowers.
These were first knitted with the idea of an Easter decoration but we quickly
realized that they could stay out all year.

EASTER TIP: *Let the woodpecker guard the marzipan eggs.*

CHARACTERISTICS: A speckled lime-green bird with a star motif and red head. Inspired by the green woodpecker. The red crosses on the tail and rump are embroidered after the bird has been knitted and filled. The red stitches were originally knit with lime-green.

WOODPECKER

MATERIALS

Yarn: CYCA #3 (DK weight) Schachenmayr Merino Extrafine 120 DK, 100% wool (131 yd/ 120 m / 50 g)
Colors: Blue 00151, Lime-Green 00175, Red 00131
Needles: U.S. size 0-2.5 / 2-3 mm, set of 5 dpn
Gauge: 30 sts and 40 rnds in 4 x 4 in / 10 x 10 cm. Adjust needle size to obtain correct gauge if necessary.

With Lime-Green, CO 14 sts and divide onto 4 dpn: 4 + 3 + 4 + 3. Join to work in the round.

NOTE: The red stitches on the tail and stomach are embroidered on later.

TAIL

Work 21 rnds following the chart on this page.

Continue, following the Basic Pattern on page 22 except as indicated below:

RUMP

This pattern varies from the Basic Pattern on Rnd 1:
Rnd 1: (K3, inc 1, k1, inc 1 in the same st as the previous inc, k3) 2 times.
Rnd 2: K18.
Rnd 3: (K1, inc 1, k7, inc 1, k1) 2 times.
Rnd 4: K22.
Rnd 5: (K1, inc 1, k9, inc 1, k1) 2 times.
Rnd 6: K26.
Rnd 7: (K1, inc 1, k11, inc 1, k1) 2 times.
Rnd 8: K30.
Rnd 9: (K1, inc 1, k13, inc 1, k1) 2 times.
Rnd 10: K34.
Rnd 11: (K1, inc 1, k15, inc 1, k1) 2 times.
Rnd 12: K38.

Now continue, following the Basic Pattern on page 22 to the head.

HEAD

The instructions for the head vary from the Basic Pattern on Rnd 2.

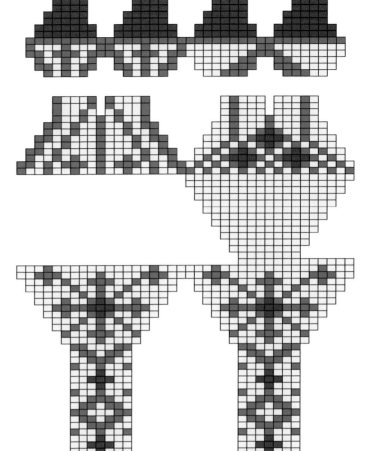

Rnd 1: K20.
Rnd 2: K1, inc 1, k4, inc 1, k2, inc 1, k3, inc 1, k1, inc 1, k3, inc 1, k1, inc 1, k4, inc 1, k1.
Rnd 3: K28.
Rnd 4: (K1, inc 1, k5, inc 1, k1) 4 times.
Rnd 5: K36.
Rnd 6: K36.
Rnd 7: (K1, k2tog, k3, k2tog, k1) 4 times.
Rnd 8: K28.
Rnd 9: (K1, k2tog, k1, k2tog, k1) 4 times.
Rnd 10: K20.
Rnd 11: (K1, k2tog, k4, k2tog, k1) 2 times.
Rnd 12: K16.
Rnd 13: (K1, k2tog, k1) around.

Cut yarn and draw end through rem 12 sts.
Flatten the tail and sew the end at the cast-on row, making sure that the top and bottom sides are correctly oriented.
Stretch the body well and tighten any stitches that are loose.
Block by gently steam pressing under a damp pressing cloth. Fill the bird and sew the hole at top of head.
Crochet the beak and sew on the eyes. This bird has a red beak and black eyes.

CHARACTERISTICS: Yellow and blue bird with pink head and pink stitches embroidered on the body.

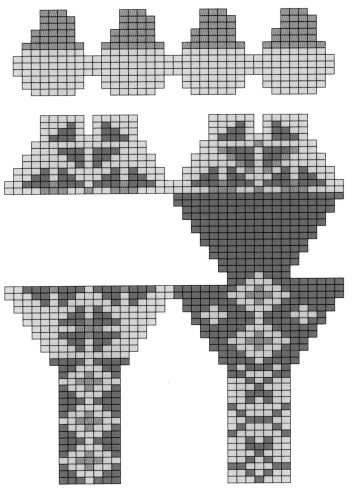

EASTER

MATERIALS

Yarn: CYCA #3 (DK weight) Schachenmayr Merino Extrafine 120 DK, 100% wool (131 yd/120 m / 50 g)
Colors: Blue 00151, Pink 00137, Yellow 00121
Needles: U.S. size 0-2.5 / 2-3 mm, set of 5 dpn
Gauge: 30 sts and 40 rnds in 4 x 4 in / 10 x 10 cm.
Adjust needle size to obtain correct gauge if necessary.

NOTE: The pink stitches on the tail, rump, and breast are embroidered with duplicate stitch after the bird has been knitted.

With Blue, CO 14 sts and divide onto 4 dpn: 4 + 3 + 4 + 3. Join to work in the round.

TAIL

Work 18 rnds following the chart on this page.

Continue, following the Basic Pattern on page 22 and the chart on this page except as indicated below.

RUMP

This pattern varies from the Basic Pattern on Rnd 1:
Rnd 1: K1, inc 1, k5, inc 1, k1, inc 1, k6, inc 1, k1.
Rnd 2: K18.
Rnd 3: (K1, inc 1, k7, inc 1, k1) 2 times.
Rnd 4: K22.

Rnd 5: (K1, inc 1, k9, inc 1, k1) 2 times.
Rnd 6: K26.
Rnd 7: (K1, inc 1, k11, inc 1, k1) 2 times.
Rnd 8: K30.
Rnd 9: (K1, inc 1, k13, inc 1, k1) 2 times.
Rnd 10: K34.
Rnd 11: (K1, inc 1, k15, inc 1, k1) 2 times.
Rnd 12: K38.

Now continue, following the Basic Pattern on page 22.

Cut yarn and draw end through rem 12 sts.
Flatten the tail and sew the end at the cast-on row, making sure that the top and bottom sides are correctly oriented.
Stretch the body well and tighten any stitches that are loose.
When the head doesn't have any patterning, you need to be careful when you fill it so it's not too big in relation to the body.
Block by gently steam pressing under a damp pressing cloth. Fill the bird and sew the hole at top of head to close.
Crochet the beak and sew on the eyes. This bird has a pink beak and dark blue eyes to match the head.

CHARACTERISTICS: Easy to recognize by the large tulip patterning over the back and wings but difficult to spot when hiding in red and yellow tulips—hence the name.

TULIP

MATERIALS

Yarn: CYCA #3 (DK weight) Schachenmayr Merino Extrafine 120 DK, 100% wool (131 yd/120 m / 50 g)
Colors: Red 00131 and Yellow 00120; small amount of Black 00199 for beak
Needles: U.S. size 0-2.5 / 2-3 mm, set of 5 dpn
Gauge: 30 sts and 40 rnds in 4 x 4 in / 10 x 10 cm.
Adjust needle size to obtain correct gauge if necessary.

With Red, CO 14 sts and divide onto 4 dpn: 4 + 3 + 4 + 3. Join to work in the round.

TAIL

Work 18 rnds following the chart on this page.

Continue, following the Basic Pattern on page 22 and the chart on this page except as indicated below.

RUMP

This pattern varies from the Basic Pattern on Rnd 3:
Rnd 1: (K1, inc 1, k5, inc 1, k1) 2 times.
Rnd 2: K18.
Rnd 3: K1, inc 1, k7, inc 1, k2, inc 1, k7, inc 1, k1.
Rnd 4: K22.
Rnd 5: (K1, inc 1, k9, inc 1, k1) 2 times.

Rnd 6: K26.
Rnd 7: (K1, inc 1, k11, inc 1, k1) 2 times.
Rnd 8: K30.
Rnd 9: (K1, inc 1, k13, inc 1, k1) 2 times.
Rnd 10: K34.
Rnd 11: (K1, inc 1, k15, inc 1, k1) 2 times.
Rnd 12: K38.

Now continue, following the Basic Pattern on page 22.

Cut yarn and draw end through rem 12 sts.
Flatten the tail and sew the end at the cast-on row, making sure that the top and bottom sides are correctly oriented.
Stretch the body well and tighten any stitches that are loose.
Block by gently steam pressing under a damp pressing cloth. Fill the bird and sew the hole at top of head to close.
Crochet the beak and sew on the eyes. This bird has a black beak and black eyes.

CHARACTERISTICS: Easily recognizable flower pattern over the tail, rump, and breast.

CROCUS

MATERIALS

Yarn: CYCA #3 (DK weight) Schachenmayr Merino Extrafine 120 DK, 100% wool (131 yd/120 m / 50 g)
Colors: White 00101, Yellow 00120, Green 00172, Pink 00137; small amount of Red 00131 for beak
Needles: U.S. size 0-2.5 / 2-3 mm, set of 5 dpn
Gauge: 30 sts and 40 rnds in 4 x 4 in / 10 x 10 cm.
Adjust needle size to obtain correct gauge if necessary.

With White, CO 14 sts and divide onto 4 dpn: 4 + 3 + 4 + 3. Join to work in the round.

TAIL

Work 25 rnds following the chart on this page.

Continue, following the Basic Pattern on page 22 and the chart on this page.

Cut yarn and draw end through rem 12 sts.
Flatten the tail and sew the end at the cast-on row, making sure that the top and bottom sides are correctly oriented.
Stretch the body well and tighten any stitches that are loose.
Block by gently steam pressing under a damp pressing cloth. Fill the bird and sew the hole at top of head.
Crochet the beak and sew on the eyes. This bird has a red beak and red eyes.

CHARACTERISTICS: Spring green bird with red star patterns on the breast and back. When observed from above, the star motif on the head is visible. Can be confused with the woodpecker but is more closely related to the long-tailed tit.

STARCAP

MATERIALS

Yarn: CYCA #3 (DK weight) Schachenmayr Merino Extrafine 120 DK, 100% wool (131 yd/ 120 m / 50 g)

Colors: Dark Green 00171, Light Green 00175, Red 00131; small amount of Black 00199 for beak

Needles: U.S. size 0-2.5 / 2-3 mm, set of 5 dpn

Gauge: 30 sts and 40 rnds in 4 x 4 in / 10 x 10 cm. Adjust needle size to obtain correct gauge if necessary.

With Dark Green, CO 14 sts and divide onto 4 dpn: 4 + 3 + 4 + 3. Join to work in the round.

TAIL

Work 28 rnds following the chart on this page.

Continue, following the Basic Pattern on page 22 and the chart on this page except as indicated below.

RUMP

This pattern varies from the Basic Pattern on Rnd 3:

Rnd 1: (K1, inc 1, k5, inc 1, k1) 2 times.
Rnd 2: K18.
Rnd 3: (Inc 1, k8, inc 1, k1) 2 times.
Rnd 4: K22.
Rnd 5: (K1, inc 1, k9, inc 1, k1) 2 times.
Rnd 6: K26.
Rnd 7: (K1, inc 1, k11, inc 1, k1) 2 times.
Rnd 8: K30.
Rnd 9: (K1, inc 1, k13, inc 1, k1) 2 times.
Rnd 10: K34.
Rnd 11: (K1, inc 1, k15, inc 1, k1) 2 times.
Rnd 12: K38.

Now continue, following the Basic Pattern on page 22.

Cut yarn and draw end through rem 12 sts.

Flatten the tail and sew the end at the cast-on row, making sure that the top and bottom sides are correctly oriented.

Stretch the body well and tighten any stitches that are loose.

When the head is knitted with minimal patterning, you need to be careful when you fill it so it's not too big in relation to the body.

Block by gently steam pressing under a damp pressing cloth. Fill the bird and sew the hole at top of head to close.

Crochet the beak and sew on the eyes. This bird has a black beak and black eyes.

An overview of most of the spring birds.

Characteristics: Orange patterning covers the body.

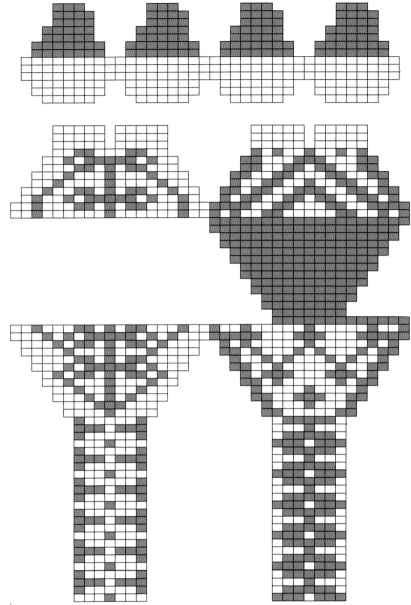

LILY

MATERIALS

Yarn: CYCA #3 (DK weight) Schachenmayr Merino Extrafine 120 DK, 100% wool (131 yd/120 m / 50 g)
Colors: Orange 00125 and White 00101; small amount of Black 00199 for beak
Needles: U.S. size 0-2.5 / 2-3 mm, set of 5 dpn
Gauge: 30 sts and 40 rnds in 4 x 4 in / 10 x 10 cm.
Adjust needle size to obtain correct gauge if necessary.

With Orange, CO 14 sts and divide onto 4 dpn: 4 + 3 + 4 + 3. Join to work in the round.

TAIL

Work 24 rnds following the chart on this page.

Continue, following the Basic Pattern on page 22 and the chart on this page.

Cut yarn and draw end through rem 12 sts.
Flatten the tail and sew the end at the cast-on row, making sure that the top and bottom sides are correctly oriented.
Stretch the body well and tighten any stitches that are loose.
When the head is knitted without stranded patterning, you need to be careful when you fill it so it's not too big relative to the body.
Block by gently steam pressing under a damp pressing cloth. Fill the bird and sew the hole at top of head to close.
Crochet the beak and sew on the eyes. This bird has a black beak and black eyes.

143

CHARACTERISTICS: This bird has a dark blue crown and stomach in contrast to the delicate flower-inspired pattern over the tail rump, back, and breast. It's actually closely related to the better-known green woodpecker. This bluecap is sitting on and tending its eggs under a decorative glass bell.

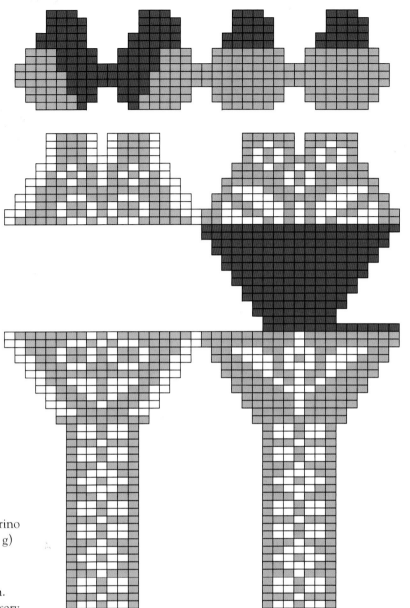

BLUECAP

MATERIALS

Yarn: CYCA #3 (DK weight) Schachenmayr Merino Extrafine 120 DK, 100% wool (131 yd/120 m / 50 g)
Colors: Green 00174, White 00101, Blue 00153
Needles: U.S. size 0-2.5 / 2-3 mm, set of 5 dpn
Gauge: 30 sts and 40 rnds in 4 x 4 in / 10 x 10 cm.
Adjust needle size to obtain correct gauge if necessary.

With Green, CO 14 sts and divide onto 4 dpn: 4 + 3 + 4 + 3. Join to work in the round.

TAIL

Work 25 rnds following the chart on this page.

Continue, following the Basic Pattern on page 22 and the chart on this page.

DETAILS ON HEAD

The blue yarn is stranded on the wrong side when you knit the green. Work 3 to 4 stitches and twist the blue yarn with the green on the wrong side. Don't twist the

strands at the same point on the next round because the blue yarn will start showing through on the right side. Do the same with the green when working more than 4 stitches at the blue back neck.

Cut yarn and draw end through rem 12 sts.
Flatten the tail and sew the end at the cast-on row, making sure that the top and bottom sides are correctly oriented.
Stretch the body well and tighten any stitches that are loose.
Block by gently steam pressing under a damp pressing cloth. Fill the bird and sew the hole at top of head to close.
Crochet the beak and sew on the eyes. This bird has a blue beak and blue eyes.

145

Chapter 9

RARE BIRDS
OF PARADISE

Pl. IX.

These birds, inspired by antique Christmas tree birds, are knitted with Anchor Mouliné 6-ply embroidery thread (100% cotton) and needles U.S. size 000 / 1.5 mm. You need two hanks of embroidery thread to knit the body.

Gather all you need in terms of beads, sequins, and feathers and see what happens. We limited ourselves to embroidery on the rump and back/wings. Sometimes the feathers inspire the color for the body and at other times it's the sequins, or sometimes the feathers and sequins are so fine together that the body comes last.

It is hard to stop knitting these birds, especially if you have a lot of feathers and sequins on hand—finally you have a use for them!

The birds of paradise are knitted with shorter tails than the other birds but otherwise worked with the same basic pattern. You won't need to sew the end of the tail together after the bird is knitted. Just fill the bird and then close the hole at the top of the head. The feathers are dipped in glue and inserted into the hole in the tail.

BASIC PATTERN FOR THE BIRDS OF PARADISE

MATERIALS

Yarn: CYCA #0 (lace weight) Anchor Mouliné 6-ply embroidery thread (100% cotton, 9 yd/8 m per hank), 2 hanks

Needles: U.S. size 000 / 1.5 mm, set of 5 dpn

Gauge: 30 sts and 40 rnds in 4 x 4 in / 10 x 10 cm. Adjust needle size to obtain correct gauge if necessary.

CO 10 sts and divide onto 4 dpn: 3 + 2 + 3 + 2. Join to work in the round.

TAIL

Rnd 1: K10.
Rnd 2: K10.
Rnd 3: (K1, inc 1, k3, inc 1, k1) 2 times.

Rnd 4: K14.
Rnd 5: K14.
Rnd 6: (K1, inc 1, k5, inc 1, k1) 2 times.
Rnd 7: K18.
Rnd 8: K18.

Continue by following the instructions in the Basic Pattern (page 22), beginning on Rnd 3 for the rump.

Fill the bird. Sew the hole at top of head closed but leave the tail end open for the feathers. You might want to embroider the bird before you glue on the feathers because the embroidery yarn could get caught in the tail as you work—very frustrating!

SEWING ON THE SEQUINS

1   We sew the sequins very closely together so they overlap. These are sewn on in horizontal rows.

2   When you've attached a sequin, insert the needle up once again into that sequin and then stitch into the previously-placed sequin, and, next, into the nearest one in the row below. That way the sequins will be firmly and closely attached.

3   You can also begin by marking the sequin lines following the increase lines on the rump and decrease lines on the breast by sewing a line of sequins from the tail up, on both sides of the body.

4   When you've finished sewing the lines on each side, all you need to do is fill in between the lines with sequins.

ATTACHING THE FEATHERS

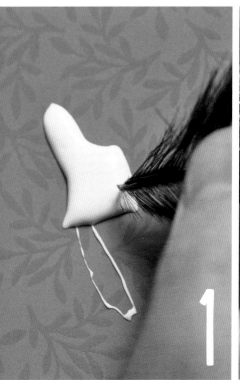 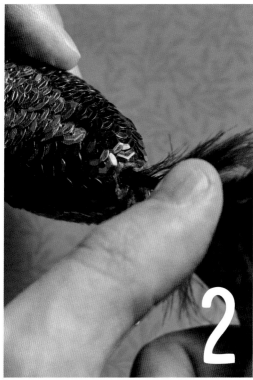 

1 Spread a little all-purpose white glue on a piece of paper and dip the ends of the feathers into the glue.

2 Stick the feathers into the hole in the tail.

3 Continue until the bird has as many feathers are you like or there is no more room.

CHARACTERISTICS: Tail and head in shades of red. Conspicuous back and wing
sections heavily covered with sequins and beads in various shades of yellow.

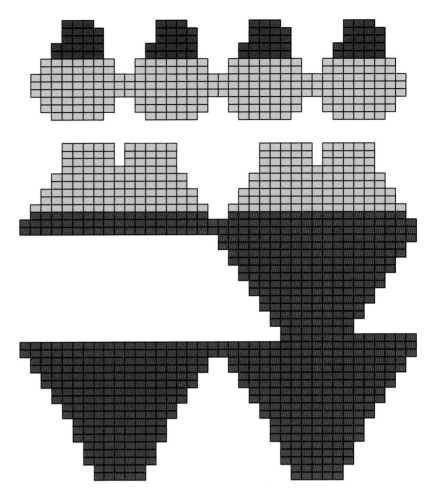

YELLOW BIRD

MATERIALS

Yarn: CYCA #0 (lace weight) Anchor Mouliné
6-ply embroidery thread (100% cotton,
9 yd/8 m per hank)
Colors: Rust Red 341, Old Rose 882, Red 47;
small amount Black 403 for beak
Other Materials:
2 black beads for the eyes
gold sequins
gold beads
gold post sequins
red-brown feathers
Needles: U.S. size 000 / 1.5 mm, set of 5 dpn
Gauge: 30 sts and 40 rnds in 4 x 4 in / 10 x 10 cm.
Adjust needle size to obtain correct gauge if necessary.

*With Rust Red, CO 10 sts and divide onto 4 dpn: 3 + 2 + 3
+ 2. Join to work in the round.*

Continue, following the Basic Pattern on page 151 and
the chart on this page.

Fill the bird. Sew the hole at top of head closed but leave
the tail end open.

Sew two lines of gold sequins at the sides over the increase and decrease lines. Begin at the tail and stop where
the color shifts from rust to rose. Sew on horizontal lines
with the post sequins from the tail and up to the rose section. Now you've marked the sides and just have to fill in
with sequins and beads. Work from the tail up.

Dip the tips of the feathers into the all-purpose glue and
insert them one by one into the tail.

Sew on the black eyes and crochet a black beak.

For the bird shown here, the sequins are sewn on over the
increase and decrease lines at the sides. When sewing on
the sequins from the rump up, you can "cover the bird
with feathers." The post sequins are sewn on three-by-
three in horizontal rows over each other.

CHARACTERISTICS: At first glance, you will only notice the mint-green head and a yellow-colored back. If you look more closely at the bird, you'll see that the wings are shimmering black, purple, blue, and green. The long tail has metallic green tones.

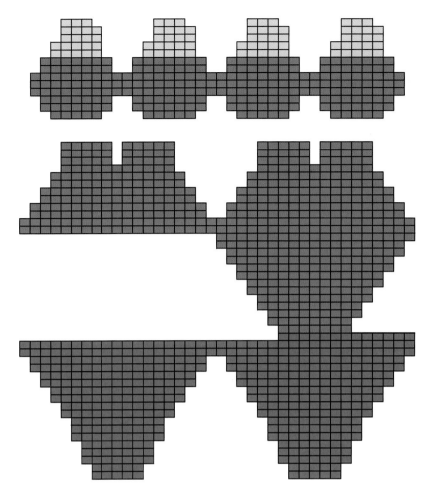

GREENTAIL

MATERIALS

Yarn: CYCA #0 (lace weight) Anchor Mouliné 6-ply
embroidery thread (100% cotton, 9 yd/8 m per hank)
Colors: Blue 132, Green 217, Mint 1092; small amount
Blue for beak
Other Materials:
2 blue beads for the eyes
gold sequins + black sequins that shimmer purple, green,
and blue
black tail feathers with metallic green tones.
Needles: U.S. size 000 / 1.5 mm, set of 5 dpn
Gauge: 30 sts and 40 rnds in 4 x 4 in / 10 x 10 cm.
Adjust needle size to obtain correct gauge if necessary.

*With Blue, CO 10 sts and divide onto 4 dpn: 3 + 2 + 3 + 2.
Join to work in the round.*

Continue, following the Basic Pattern on page 151 and
the chart on this page.

Fill the bird. Sew the hole at top of head closed but leave
the tail end open.
Mark the increase and decrease lines with a row of dark
sequins on each side of the body. Begin at the tail and
stop at the base of the neck. Working from the tail up,
continue up the curved line with three more rows of the
same dark sequins. When you have four lines of sequins
over the wings on each side of the bird's body, fill in the
empty triangle on the back with gold sequins.
Dip the tips of the feathers into the all-purpose glue and
insert them one by one into the tail.
Sew on the blue eyes and crochet a blue beak.

CHARACTERISTICS: Can be confused with a bird of paradise because of the long fluttery tail. The back and wings are shiny pink. Pink eyes and burgundy beak. Often flies up into wedding cakes and has a tendency to nest close to party venues.

DECORATING TIP: *There is a high glamour factor among birds of paradise because they are always dressed in their finest. They are best for big celebrations and weddings, so incorporate these birds in the most elegant flower arrangements.*

THE WHITE I DO I DO I DO

MATERIALS

Yarn: CYCA #0 (lace weight) Anchor Mouliné 6-ply embroidery thread (100% cotton, 9 yd/8 m per hank)
Colors: White 1, 2 hanks; small amount Burgundy for beak
Other Materials:
2 pink beads for the eyes
pink sequins
long white ostrich feathers
Needles: U.S. size 000 / 1.5 mm, set of 5 dpn
Gauge: 30 sts and 40 rnds in 4 x 4 in / 10 x 10 cm.
Adjust needle size to obtain correct gauge if necessary.

With White, CO 10 sts and divide onto 4 dpn: 3 + 2 + 3 + 2. Join to work in the round.

Continue, following the Basic Pattern on page 151.

Fill the bird. Sew the hole at top of head closed but leave the tail end open.
Cover the back and wings with pink sequins, sewing them on in horizontal rows from the tail up to the shoulders. The lines begin and end at the increase and decrease lines on the rump and back.
Dip the tips of the feathers into the all-purpose glue and insert them one by one into the tail.
Sew on the pink eyes and crochet a burgundy beak.

CHARACTERISTICS: Blue-green bird with a conspicuously long tail, blue crown, and gold-edged wings. Might be confused with its distant relative, the peacock, but only if you see it in a picture. In reality, it is only 9¾ in / 25 cm long, including the tail.

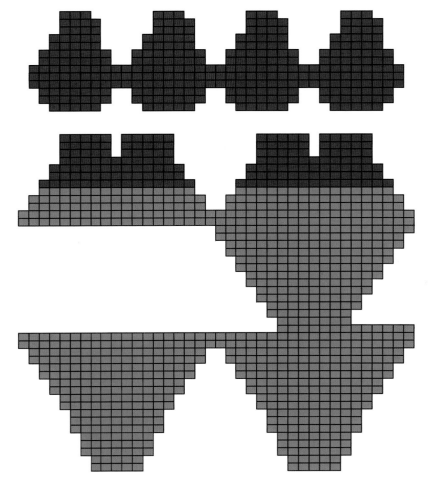

ROYAL BLUEBIRD

MATERIALS

Yarn: CYCA #0 (lace weight) Anchor Mouliné 6-ply embroidery thread (100% cotton, 9 yd/8 m per hank)
Colors: Green 243 and Blue 164; small amount Light Green 1097 for beak
Other Materials:
2 green beads for the eyes
13 blue beads
blue and copper sequins
1 peacock feather
Needles: U.S. size 000 / 1.5 mm, set of 5 dpn
Gauge: 30 sts and 40 rnds in 4 x 4 in / 10 x 10 cm.
Adjust needle size to obtain correct gauge if necessary.

With Green, CO 10 sts and divide onto 4 dpn: 3 + 2 + 3 + 2. Join to work in the round.

Continue, following the Basic Pattern on page 151 and the chart on this page.

Fill the bird. Sew the hole at top of head closed but leave the tail end open.

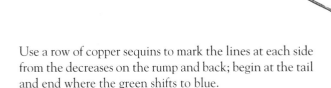

Use a row of copper sequins to mark the lines at each side from the decreases on the rump and back; begin at the tail and end where the green shifts to blue.
Fill the space between the copper lines on the back with blue sequins.
Dip the tip of the main feather into the all-purpose glue and insert into the tail. The thinner feathers can be trimmed off and then glued to lie underneath the main feather.
Sew on the green eyes and crochet a green beak. Thread the 13 blue beads onto a thin cord and tie into a ring. Sew crown onto top of bird's head.

CHARACTERISTICS: This bird is four shades of green with yellow interspersed in the tail. Glistening light green wings. Almost impossible to observe since it nests in trees with matching leaf colors.

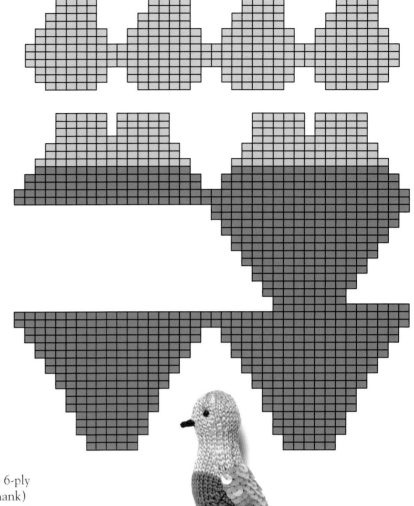

RUFFLE-TAIL

MATERIALS

Yarn: CYCA #0 (lace weight) Anchor Mouliné 6-ply embroidery thread (100% cotton, 9 yd/8 m per hank)

Colors: Light Green 1097 and Dark Green 227; small amount Black 403 for beak

Other Materials:
2 black beads for the eyes
light green sequins
about 1¼ in / 3 cm of the widest part of two green feathers and some pheasant neck feathers (as for fly-tying)

Needles: U.S. size 000 / 1.5 mm, set of 5 dpn

Gauge: 30 sts and 40 rnds in 4 x 4 in / 10 x 10 cm.
Adjust needle size to obtain correct gauge if necessary.

With Dark Green, CO 10 sts and divide onto 4 dpn: 3 + 2 + 3 + 2. Join to work in the round.

Continue, following the Basic Pattern on page 151 and the chart on this page.

Fill the bird. Sew the hole at top of head closed but leave the tail end open.
Begin sewing the sequins along the increase lines on the rump and along the decrease lines on the breast and back. End where the dark green shifts to light green.

Fill in the space between the lines of sequins on the back with light green sequins.
Dip the tips of the feathers into the all-purpose glue and insert one by one into the tail.
For the ruffle tail, we found sequins that matched the color of the back neck and head. When you are knitting a similar bird, you might want to start with sequins that you have on hand and match the yarn, or vice versa. This is one of the aspects that make knitting birds of paradise exciting.
Sew on the black eyes and crochet a black beak.

163

CHARACTERISTICS: A seldom-seen bird of paradise with shiny silver wings and a long, elegant brown and white tail surrounded by yellow-spotted black feathers. The long tail feathers make this a very elegant bird. Attach to a branch so the tail shows to the fullest extent.

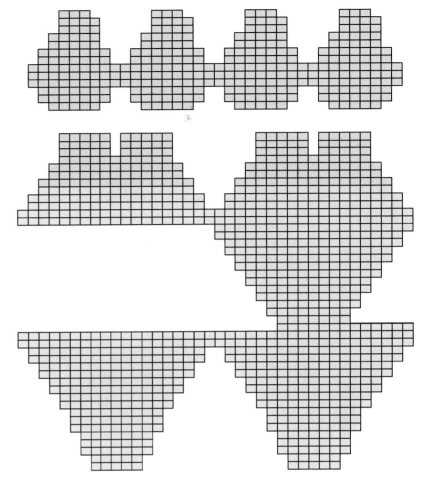

SILVER WINGS

MATERIALS

Yarn: CYCA #0 (lace weight) Anchor Mouliné 6-ply embroidery thread (100% cotton, 9 yd/8 m per hank)
Colors: Gray 397 and Yellow 290; small amount Black 403 for beak
Other Materials:
2 black beads for the eyes
silver sequins
pheasant neck feathers (as for fly-tying) + long black/white feathers
Needles: U.S. size 000 / 1.5 mm, set of 5 dpn
Gauge: 30 sts and 40 rnds in 4 x 4 in / 10 x 10 cm.
Adjust needle size to obtain correct gauge if necessary.

With Gray, CO 10 sts and divide onto 4 dpn: 3 + 2 + 3 + 2.
Join to work in the round.

Continue, following the Basic Pattern on page 151 and the chart on this page.

Fill the bird. Sew the hole at top of head closed but leave the tail end open.
Begin sewing the sequins along the increase lines on the rump and along the decrease lines on the breast and back, up to the head.

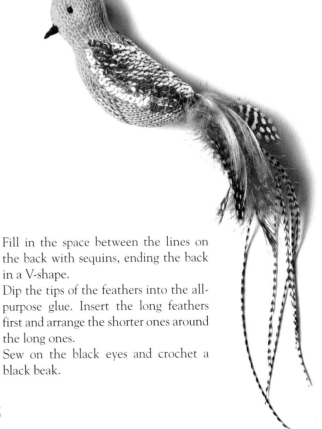

Fill in the space between the lines on the back with sequins, ending the back in a V-shape.
Dip the tips of the feathers into the all-purpose glue. Insert the long feathers first and arrange the shorter ones around the long ones.
Sew on the black eyes and crochet a black beak.

CHARACTERISTICS: Long brown tail feathers that stick out from deep rose downy feathers around the rump. Both the top and bottom of the rump are a shimmering deep rose edged with beads. This bird doesn't look like it can manage to leave its eggs. The top of its head is purple, crowned with a ring of beads—hence its name.

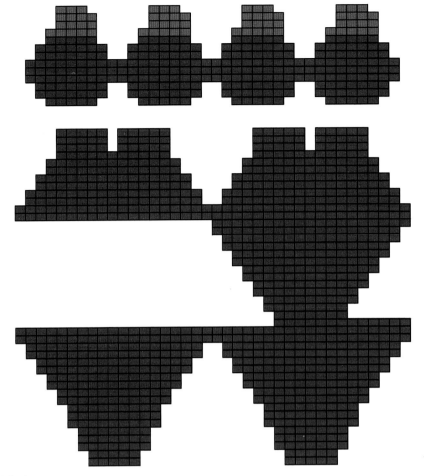

BEADED CROWN

MATERIALS

Yarn: CYCA #0 (lace weight) Anchor Mouliné 6-ply embroidery thread (100% cotton, 9 yd/8 m per hank)

Colors: 2 hanks Red 9046; small amount of Purple 99 + Gray 397 held together for top of head and beak

Other Materials:
2 blue beads for the eyes
dark pink sequins for the rump
9 white beads paired with light pink sequins and smaller yellow and silver beads to string between them
purple-dyed chicken feathers and red-brown long pointed feathers

Needles: U.S. size 000 / 1.5 mm, set of 5 dpn

Gauge: 30 sts and 40 rnds in 4 x 4 in / 10 x 10 cm.
Adjust needle size to obtain correct gauge if necessary.

With Red, CO 10 sts and divide onto 4 dpn: 3 + 2 + 3 + 2. Join to work in the round.

Continue, following the Basic Pattern on page 151 and the chart on this page.

Fill the bird. Sew the hole at top of head closed but leave the tail end open.
Baste an elegant line over the back and in a soft curve down over the lower rump. Sew sequins around and

around from the opening for the feathers and up to the basting / tacking line. Edge the sequined area with white beads alternating with yellow beads. The number of beads will depend on the gauge of the knitting. For the crown, string the white beads, sequins, and small silver beads on a string and tie into a ring. Sew crown around the edge of the purple crown of the head.

Dip the tips of the long feathers and insert them before gluing in the shorter feathers around the long ones.
Sew on the blue eyes and crochet a purple/gray beak.

CHARACTERISTICS: A small woodpecker related to the bird of paradise. Golden back and red-orange tail feathers with black lines.

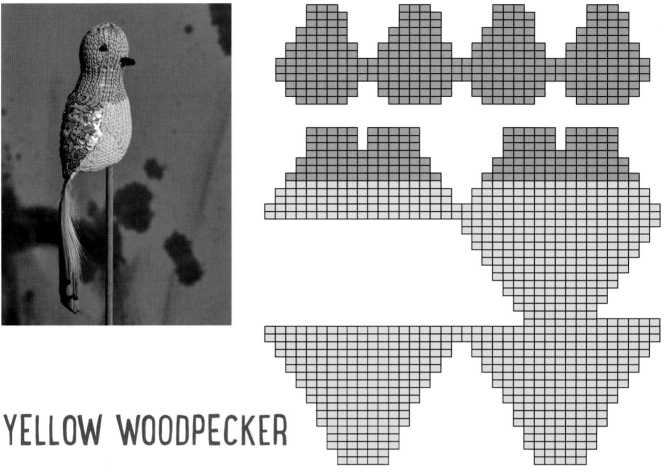

YELLOW WOODPECKER

MATERIALS

Yarn: CYCA #0 (lace weight) Anchor Mouliné 6-ply embroidery thread (100% cotton, 9 yd/8 m per hank)
Colors: Yellow 297 and Green 858; small amount of Black 403 for the beak
Other Materials:
2 black beads for the eyes
gold sequins
golden pheasant back neck feathers (as used for for fly-tying)
Needles: U.S. size 000 / 1.5 mm, set of 5 dpn
Gauge: 30 sts and 40 rnds in 4 x 4 in / 10 x 10 cm.
Adjust needle size to obtain correct gauge if necessary.

With Yellow, CO 10 sts and divide onto 4 dpn: 3 + 2 + 3 + 2. Join to work in the round.

Continue, following the Basic Pattern on page 151 and the chart on this page.

Fill the bird. Sew the hole at top of head closed but leave the tail end open.
Sew a row of sequins over the increase lines of the rump

and decrease lines of the breast and back on each side. End where the yellow shifts to green. Fill in the space between these two lines with more sequins.
Dip the tips of the feathers into the all-purpose glue and insert into the tail.
Sew on the black eyes and crochet a black beak.

CHARACTERISTICS: Don't be fooled by the name of this bird. When the bird is sitting, you'll only see a small white band at the outer edges of the wings. But when the bird flies, it reveals the spotless white undersides.

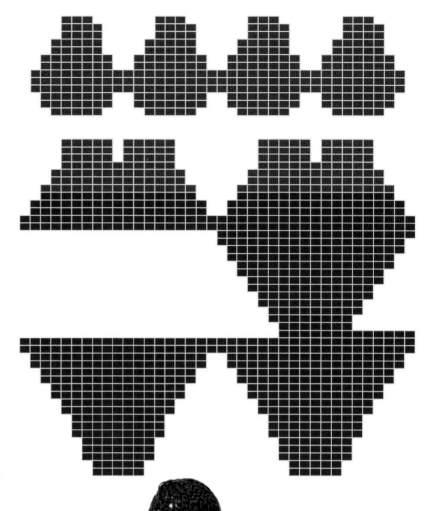

WHITE WINGS

MATERIALS

Yarn: CYCA #0 (lace weight) Anchor Mouliné 6-ply embroidery thread (100% cotton, 9 yd/8 m per hank)
Colors: Dark Blue 150 and Burgundy 44; small amount of Orange 314 for the beak
Other Materials:
2 orange beads for the eyes
brown and black sequins
white post sequins for edging the wings
golden pheasant back neck feathers (as used for for fly-tying)
Needles: U.S. size 000 / 1.5 mm, set of 5 dpn
Gauge: 30 sts and 40 rnds in 4 x 4 in / 10 x 10 cm.
Adjust needle size to obtain correct gauge if necessary.

With Dark Blue, CO 10 sts and divide onto 4 dpn: 3 + 2 + 3 + 2. Join to work in the round.

Continue, following the Basic Pattern on page 151 and the chart on this page.

Fill the bird. Sew the hole at top of head closed but leave the tail end open.

Sew a row of sequins over the increase lines of the rump and decrease lines of the breast and back on each side. Begin by marking a V-shape with black and then fill in with brown sequins all the way up to the head. Mark a line along the sides of the rump with white post sequins (see photo).
Dip the tips of the feathers into the all-purpose glue and insert into the tail.
Sew on the orange eyes and crochet an orange beak.

Make your own "Curiosity Cabinet." Inspired by the Victorian glass bells filled with dried flowers and stuffed hummingbirds, we arranged some branches with steel wire and decorated them with birds of paradise and artful flowers and leaves.

CHARACTERISTICS: Colorful, shy and rare birds.

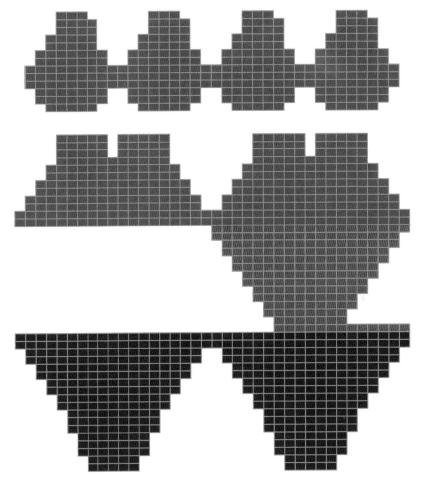

RAINBOW BIRD

MATERIALS

Yarn: CYCA #0 (lace weight) Anchor Mouliné 6-ply embroidery thread (100% cotton, 9 yd/8 m per hank)
Colors: Black 403, Red 47, Green 2018
Other Materials:
2 red beads for the eyes
black, white, dark pink, and silver sequins
brown feathers
Needles: U.S. size 000 / 1.5 mm, set of 5 dpn
Gauge: 30 sts and 40 rnds in 4 x 4 in / 10 x 10 cm.
Adjust needle size to obtain correct gauge if necessary.

With Black, CO 10 sts and divide onto 4 dpn: 3 + 2 + 3 + 2. Join to work in the round.

Continue, following the Basic Pattern on page 151 and the chart on this page.

Fill the bird. Sew the hole at top of head closed but leave the tail end open.

Sew a row of sequins over the increase lines of the rump and decrease lines of the breast and back on each side.

Begin by marking a V-shape with black and then fill in with brown sequins all the way up to the head. Mark a

line along the sides of the rump. Sew silver sequins along the increase line at the sides of the rump. Fill half of the triangle between the silver sequins with dark pink sequins. Working in a U-shape, sew white sequins along the line of decreases on the breast and back. Finally, sew a circle of black sequins in the U-shape and up to the head. Dip the tips of the feathers into the all-purpose glue and insert into the tail.
Sew on the red eyes and crochet a red beak.

173

Find some nice branches and cut them to the right height so that they'll fit under the glass bell. When the branches are the right size, set the bell on its side and trim the first branch while you clip away whatever needs to be trimmed so the branch will fit. When it fits, attach a couple of branches around the stem of the upright branch so that it will stand up well. Now the "tree" is ready for decoration.

RESOURCES

•Gudjónsson, Elsa E. "The Origins of Icelandic Knitting." *Knitting with Icelandic Wool*. Reykjavik, Iceland: Vaka-Helgafell, 2011.
•Sibbern Bøhn, Annichen. *Norsk Strikkemønstre*. Oslo, 1947. In English as *Norwegian Knitting Designs*. Seattle, Washington: Spinningwheel, 2011.

YARN SOURCES

•Schachenmayr Merino Extrafine120 DK: see www.us.schachenmayr.com for local distributors.
•Anchor Mouliné 6-ply embroidery thread: www.makeitcoats.com or substitute DMC brand—www.dmc-usa.com. You can find Anchor-DMC color conversion charts at a number of websites.
Check your local craft shop for beads, sequins, and feathers.

If you are unable to obtain any of the yarn used in this book, it can be replaced with a yarn of a similar weight and composition. Please note, however, the finished projects may vary slightly from those shown, depending on the yarn used. Try www.yarnsub.com for suggestions.

For more information on selecting or substituting yarn, contact your local yarn shop or an online store; they are familiar with all types of yarns and would be happy to help you. Additionally, the online knitting community at Ravelry.com has forums where you can post questions about specific yarns. Yarns come and go so quickly these days and there are so many beautiful yarns available.

ARNE & CARLOS YOUTUBE CHANNEL

For loads of weekly inspiration, we recommend that you subscribe to our YouTube channel. Every week, you'll find free patterns on our website that accompany our YouTube episodes. Visit www.arnecarlos.com for more information!